Courtesy of David Kliot, M.D.

THE
GENTLE BIRTH BOOK

A PRACTICAL GUIDE TO
LEBOYER FAMILY-CENTERED DELIVERY

NANCY BEREZIN

INTRODUCTION
by John W. Grover, M.D., and John S. Robey, M.D.

Simon and Schuster • New York

PUBLISHED BY SIMON AND SCHUSTER
A DIVISION OF GULF & WESTERN CORPORATION
SIMON & SCHUSTER BUILDING
ROCKEFELLER CENTER
1230 AVENUE OF THE AMERICAS
NEW YORK, NEW YORK 10020
SIMON AND SCHUSTER AND COLOPHON ARE TRADEMARKS
OF SIMON & SCHUSTER
DESIGNED BY EVE METZ
MANUFACTURED IN THE UNITED STATES OF AMERICA

2 3 4 5 6 7 8 9 10 11

LIBRARY OF CONGRESS CATALOGING IN PUBLICATION DATA

BEREZIN, NANCY, DATE.
   THE GENTLE BIRTH BOOK.

   BIBLIOGRAPHY: P.
1. NATURAL CHILDBIRTH. 2. LEBOYER, FRÉDÉRICK. 3. INFANTS (NEWBORN)
—CARE AND HYGIENE. 4. INFANTS (NEWBORN)—PSYCHOLOGY. 5. FAMILY.
I. TITLE.
RG661.B47   1980   618.4'5   79-26570

ISBN 0-671-24299-7
The author gratefully acknowledges permission to reprint excerpts from Birth Without
Violence *by Frederick Leboyer, copyright © 1975 by Alfred A. Knopf, Inc.*

FOR AMY

ACKNOWLEDGMENTS

To the dozens of families who have already chosen a gentler way of having their babies and wanted to share that experience with others;

Also, to Pat Levy and Abe Levy, M.D., for their unwavering support, and to all the other physicians who lent their time and knowledge, in particular Drs. John Franklin, William Gottschalk, Marshall H. Klaus, and John H. Kennell.

To Bernie Seeman, who taught me to love writing, Dick Stiller, who gave me the precious time in which to do it, and John Maurice, who introduced me to *Realms of the Human Unconscious.*

To my editors at Simon & Schuster, Ann-Marie Miller, Nan Talese and, most recently, Catherine Shaw, for their friendship and good advice.

To David Kliot, M.D., whose wonderful photographs enliven this book and whose personal contribution has been inestimable.

And, above all, to John W. Grover, M.D., whose approach to obstetrics combines professional expertise with deep concern for the lives of his patients and whose faith in gentle birth provided the inspiration for all that followed,

I give most sincere thanks.

CONTENTS

Introduction

Human childbirth has taken place at home, as a natural and family-centered event, for thousands of years. Only in the last century have advances in maternal-fetal management required a gradual shift from the home to the hospital for birth supervision. Medically this appears to be safer and more efficient; however, hospitalizing the laboring mother also introduces certain undesirable elements of mechanization and dehumanization. The recent rapid proliferation of technology which has proved effective in assuring the safety of birth too often succeeds in removing the woman in labor from the support of her family and friends.

Childbirth is one of life's critical passages, and new parents tend to be exceptionally vulnerable. It is relatively easy for a negative delivery experience to exert a lasting effect on their parenting capabilities. It is, similarly, surprisingly easy for a positive birth experience to reinforce and strengthen a couple's sense of mastery and competence.

Unfortunately, when a pregnant woman enters the medical caretaking system, these subtle but important aspects of management may be lost. The system is not set up to distinguish between healthy, normal physiologic processes and diseases; consequently, every laboring mother is treated as a potential medical disaster, and more refined technology is called upon to make the caretakers feel secure. As crisis-oriented care increases, human sensitivity decreases, and couples are, predictably, less happy with their birth experiences.

Discontent with medical caretaking is being expressed vigorously as expectant parents and the general public become aware of how fulfilling an uncomplicated birth experience can be. Conscious, shared, and more "natural" childbearing is sought after. Views that expectant parents should have some elements of choice and control over the process are frequently heard and help account for the burgeoning interest in alternative birth centers and home delivery. New relationships with the newborn baby, involving a calm, intimate "attachment" period immediately after birth, and better and more suitable postpartum learning experiences are now desired by many couples.

Yet these perceptions of the childbirth process are poles apart from the medical model; indeed, the two approaches are often antagonistic. Our own concern over the past fifteen years of obstetrical and pediatric practice has been to rationalize these divergent views and facilitate a positive experience that also meets our requirements for medical safety. By incorporating the perceived needs of the parents into our labor, delivery, and postpartum care, we have attempted to bring about changes in a manner acceptable to both sides.

We have adopted a "holistic" or overall view of childbirth, in which all aspects of the process are considered important and worth preparing for. Pregnancy and birth are seen as belonging to a period of psychological, physiologic, and social growth, part of the continuum of family growth and development. We are convinced that broad preparation for birth and parenting are valid ways of strengthening family life in a mobile society in which extended families are diminished and parenting skills hard to acquire.

We recognize that part of our commitment to the gentle birth approach is purely emotional, in that not all aspects of what we do are validated by controlled observations. We will all be happier with more objective support of Leboyer's and our own premises. However, the responses of our parents to their birth experiences has been so positive, and so ongoing, that it is easy for us to justify continuing until more conclusive data emerge.

This book explores the historical, philosophical, and theoretical background to our management of childbirth and presents it in a readable and understandable way. (Some of the recent speculation, such as that concerning the memory of and reaction to primal experiences, remains highly controversial.) Preparations for family-centered birth are discussed, and the events that take place during and after a gentle delivery are described in detail. Couples planning to have children may thus gain a better understanding of what to look for and what kind of questions to ask when seeking this kind of care.

What it does best of all, however, is to show in a variety of ways that having a baby need not be a computerized, space-age-instrumented, and dehumanized medical procedure. In fact, the process of birth can once again become a life-validating experience from which all emerge as more understanding, confident, and competent human beings.

JOHN W. GROVER, M.D.
JOHN S. ROBEY, M.D.

Foreword

In August of 1975, a short time after I first heard the name Leboyer, my first child, a daughter, was born.

All that summer I pelvic-rocked endlessly and practiced my Lamaze breathing. But prepared as I was for the event of birth, nothing could have prepared me for its aftermath. When Amy finally emerged, after more than a day of on-again, off-again contractions, she was red-faced and howling. It was a noise we were to hear frequently during the months that followed.

Home from the hospital, I thumbed helplessly through my growing library of reference books. All of my friends' babies seemed to suck vigorously and sleep three or four hours between feedings. Mine, despite nursing on demand, rocking, and generous use of an orthodontic pacifier, would not be comforted. What was I doing wrong?

"Relax," said my pediatrician. "She's a dramatic baby. It will pass."

Relax? How could I? My child was in pain. I felt clumsy, inexperienced, a failure as a mother. My husband was equally tense; we quarreled frequently and over trivialities. Amy, sensing the tension, cried even harder.

Luckily, time passes quickly with a new baby. By the fifth month, as the pediatrician had predicted, the worst of the crisis was over. Amy today is a sturdy, laughing four-year-old, and the day-to-day business of living with her has all but erased the memory of those difficult early weeks.

"All but. . . ." How much easier for baby *and* parents to have nothing but pleasant memories to look back upon. And this can happen.

Each birth is a new beginning, and every beginning is different. Thanks to modern obstetrical techniques and the benign influence of childbirth education, most deliveries today (even first deliveries) are relatively quick and painless affairs. Many babies emerge peacefully, even without the innovations described in this book. But many others do not.

Numb from the battering they receive in the birth canal, senses swamped by the bright lights and din of the operating room in which they are delivered, these infants resort to the only means available to them to express their misery. They cry—and cry—and cry. And in crying, they seal themselves off from contact with their parents, who become defensive and perhaps a little bit angry as well.

Where is the ecstatic experience for which they've been prepared? Can this squawking bit of protoplasm really be theirs? No, there must be some mistake. This baby doesn't want their cuddling. He doesn't even know who they are! The feeling of disappointment, of letdown, is immense.

I know.

Still, when I was assigned to write an article about gentle childbirth, I was skeptical. "You wouldn't catch me having a baby in the dark," I crowed. But then a number of things happened. First, I read Leboyer's *Birth Without Violence*. Then I met John Grover, and I talked with other physicians who had incorporated nonviolent techniques into their practices. And, finally, I saw the babies and heard from the parents what the experience had meant to them all as a family.

And I knew I had to write this book.

Because a gentle childbirth can change the picture for everyone involved in the care of an infant. Until humanity has perfected itself, some babies will always emerge, as mine did, more "battered" than others. But they don't have to remain that way.

A child who is allowed a few moments of peace to recover from his trauma, regain his momentum, and come to grips with the demands of his new environment will quickly learn that the world

I gave my love a cherry
　　that has no stone;
I gave my love a chicken
　　that has no bone;
I gave my love a ring
　　that has no end;
I gave my love a baby
　　with no crying . . .

"The Riddle Song"
(probable origin:
Colonial America)

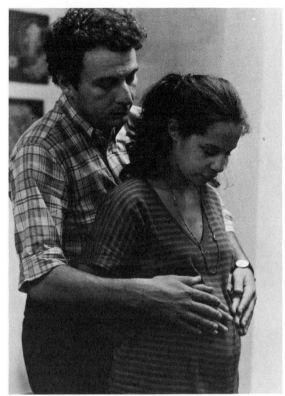

Courtesy of Pat Levy,
Lamaze-Leboyer Childbirth Education Center

1 . . . And Baby Makes Three

Childbearing has always been associated with change. Twentieth-century childbearing has become, in addition, an exercise in decision making. As the expectant mother's body alters to accommodate the developing fetus and prepare for its birth, both parents-to-be set about making a place—in their home and their consciousness—for the newest family member.

In great-grandmother's day, few choices were involved. Most

babies were delivered at home, with a midwife attending and possibly a doctor on call for emergencies. If the woman's husband was not actually present he was at least close at hand, as were older siblings, other relatives, and often friends as well. At birth the infant was immediately placed at her mother's breast to nurse. If the mother needed rest, an army of caretakers stood ready to take over the household chores, cook the meals, or cuddle and rock the baby. In this cozy setting, books on infant and child care were almost nonexistent. With so much family support, they weren't needed.

Of course, the specter of illness and death loomed darkly over this otherwise idyllic scene. For every hundred babies born at the turn of the century, one mother died. Even twenty-five years ago, perinatal and infant death rates were approximately 50 percent higher than they are today. If technology has dehumanized the event of birth and generally complicated our lives, it has also saved us from the far greater tragedy of maternal and infant death that was commonplace a century ago.

Beneficiaries of technologic advancement, yet bereft of the security afforded by tradition, today's expectant parents face a dazzling array of options in childbirth. Should delivery take place at a large teaching hospital or smaller, local institution? Are there advantages to giving birth at home or in a so-called alternative birth center? What about anesthesia? Should the newborn be breast- or bottle-fed?

Complex questions for which conflicting viewpoints are offered. . . . The young couple clip magazine articles and telephone friends for advice, then visit their local bookstore or public library and consult the experts. Finally, a way is chosen.

ENTER DR. LEBOYER

With the publication of *Birth Without Violence* in 1975,* expectant parents found that they had yet another new idea to think about—namely, birth from the baby's point of view. Immediately, letters began pouring in to the American publisher. The book became a best seller, and the slight, soft-spoken obstetrician-author was deluged with requests for speaking engagements.

* *Pour une naissance sans violence* was released in France in 1974.

But if Leboyer's words had struck a responsive chord in the American public, the medical establishment remained unmoved. In the spring of 1975, hospitals were still reeling from the impact of the natural childbirth trend. American obstetricians, who saw themselves the target of feminist criticism for everything from the surgical prep at the outset of labor to the episiotomy at its conclusion, took one look at the new techniques and declared them absurd. Nonviolent birth seemed like just another annoying departure from accepted practice, another area for which the doctor could be called to account. Fear of malpractice litigation raised its ugly head.

The very passion and conviction with which Leboyer expressed his message struck a discordant note in the ears of men trained to trust only dry analytical data. In the absence of charts and graphs, of references, of scientific proof of any kind, the general reaction even among sympathetic physicians was skepticism.

Typical comments: "The book is too dramatic . . . he should stick to poetry." "We've already cut down anesthesia and allowed fathers into the delivery room . . . what more do these parents want?" "A nice idea . . . but birth *is* violent, and to talk about changing that is nonsense."

But gentle childbirth didn't seem like nonsense to the parents and babies involved. As for the risks, they proved in time to be no greater than with conventional delivery. On the contrary, there is already some evidence that a family-centered gentle birth may be somewhat superior medically, as well as providing a more positive emotional experience for the baby, the new parents and even the birth attendants.*

As one highly respected obstetrician described the change in atmosphere: "I enjoy doing obstetrics more now than I used to. The babies are livelier, more fun to watch. Years ago, we didn't see newborns doing such clever things."

The babies haven't changed, of course. If they weren't "doing

---

* In fairness to those early critics, it should be reemphasized that at the time the safety of Leboyer's methods was hardly self-evident. While the French obstetrician had a distinguished reputation, having delivered a thousand babies nonviolently and some ten thousand others by more standard techniques, he chose to direct his appeal to his readers' hearts, rather than to their intellect. However, as will be shown, physicians who have subsequently specialized in this approach and *have* kept statistics have found no increase whatsoever in infection, heat loss, undetected cyanosis, or other complications attributable to gentle birth procedures.

such clever things," it was because—with a few lucky exceptions —they were too doped up with medication and too intimidated by the bright lights and other excessive stimuli to want to do much of anything except sleep or cry. Certainly, babies delivered by traditional obstetrical methods didn't immediately engage in eye contact with their parents, snuggle up and suckle their mother's breast, or play in the bathtub in the delivery room!

That they often do these things during gentle deliveries is well known. Why they do them, what sort of effect this has had on the parents, and how the difference may matter in the years to come is the subject of our story.

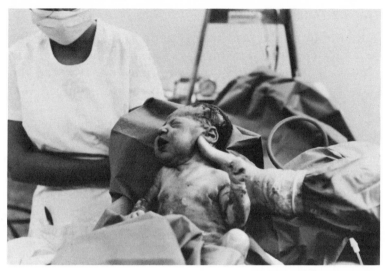

2 · Setting the Stage

When we are born, we cry that we are come to this great stage of fools.

King Lear, *IV*, 6

BACKGROUND: *Birth as Psychic Trauma*

That being born is essentially traumatic to the infant is not a new idea. For the past hundred years, psychiatrists have debated the meaning of that initial shock and the extent of its influence on all later human exchanges. Carl Jung, Sigmund Freud, and most notably Otto Rank were instrumental in focusing scientific interest on the possibility of early imprinting of painful experience on the human unconscious.

23

Rank viewed the primal separation as the prototype for all subsequent experiences involving separation and loss and saw in all phases of man's artistic and spiritual endeavor the longing to return to the bliss of the womb. Neuroses, claimed Rank, were merely varying expressions of a central psychosexual fixation on the Mother—a form of regression to the plane on which the earliest injury had taken place.

More recently, psychotherapist Arthur Janov shifted the focus to the physical struggle of birth and the complete inability of the newborn to cope with the painful sensations engendered by (among other conditions) prolonged labor, breech and posterior delivery, anoxia, strangulation by the cord, or rough handling in the immediate postpartum period.

Human beings instinctively turn away from pain, Janov notes. We flinch when our hands touch a hot stove, avert our eyes from scenes that frighten us, and routinely deny unpleasant truths about ourselves. Newborn infants, although hardly capable of verbalizing their hurt, *feel* it intensely, nevertheless.

The cortex of the newborn is functioning and has a specific electroencephalographic pattern. It is not well developed, however, so that massive input from first-line traumas cannot be circumscribed and contained by words or other symbolic representations even though the Pain may be *registered* cortically. The tremendous input from first-line traumas produces chaos in the baby brain, which is as yet inadequate to conceptualize its experience. The physical counterpart of that mental chaos is random, generalized, chaotic bodily reactions.[1]

Even without conscious awareness, birth trauma is laid down in the nervous system and "remembered organismically" in much the same way, Janov speculates, as human cells "remember" how many times to divide. When the ego moves in to repress or block this awful memory, the stage is set for neurosis.

Just as sufficient physical pain may cause a strong adult to lose consciousness, the torrent of unfiltered, unorganized sensations associated with a difficult birth results in a shutdown of responsiveness in the infant. The only cure, according to Janov, lies in bringing those buried sensations to the foreground via a reexperiencing of birth trauma in Primal therapy. Once a patient has gone back over the source of his or her pain, the neurotic defense system will at last have outlived its usefulness and can be discarded.

Obviously, Janov's views are highly controversial, even among psychiatrists. There is no denying, however, that his patients have been able to "remember" specific, painful events of the newborn period with remarkable clarity.

"I have seen a Primal," he writes, "where a woman was bunched up in a ball, gurgling, almost choking, spitting up fluid, and then straightening out and wailing like a newborn. When she came out of it, she felt that she had relived her very difficult birth, in which she was indeed filled with fluid and almost choked to death . . ."[2]

Czech psychiatrist Stanislav Grof has documented similar, stunningly accurate birth sequences in his work with LSD patients. In *Realms of the Human Unconscious* (1976), he notes that for each stage of biological birth, subjects demonstrated a corresponding psychological manifestation or "perinatal experience." Many of Grof's patients exhibited physical signs of fetal distress or moved in sequences resembling those of a baby during various stages of birth. Subjects also reported identification with embryos, fetuses, and newborn children, and experienced visions of (their mothers') genitals and breasts.

During the final stage corresponding to biological separation from the mother, patients typically showed signs of suffocation and increased muscular tension, followed by sudden inspiration, relief, and relaxation. Feelings of well-being and tranquillity engendered by a "good" birth experience could, however, be shattered by various painful stimuli, including circumcision and other surgical interventions.

Realms of the Human Unconscious makes fascinating reading. But *can* newborn babies feel physical or spiritual pain, as these psychiatrists suggest? Without more objective evidence that they have this capacity, the concept of birth trauma must be relegated to the theoretical. . . .

BACKGROUND: Birth as Sensation

Until about ten years ago, it was taken for granted that newborn infants had the good fortune to be shielded from painful stimuli by a generalized insensitivity to their environment. So effective was this barrier thought to be that circumcisions were—and still are—routinely done in the United States within twenty-four hours of birth, without anesthesia.

From the smallest community hospital to the largest regional medical center, delivery rooms were organized and staffed as operating theaters: brilliantly lit, noisy with the clanking of steel and hum of machinery, and air-conditioned for the comfort of the capped, gowned, and gloved obstetrical team. Newborn nurseries, similarly chilly and brightly lit, were outfitted with orderly rows of clear plastic cribs, making it easy for a relatively small nursing staff to monitor many tiny charges.

If babies were "monitored" rather than cuddled, if they screwed up their eyes against the light, or if they cried out in distress at being separated from their mothers, it wasn't thought to matter. After all, everyone knew that newborn babies had to cry in order to exercise their lungs, couldn't see clearly, and really didn't take much notice of their surroundings.

Or did they?

T. Berry Brazelton, chief of the child development unit at the Children's Hospital Medical Center in Boston and an internationally respected pediatrician and author, thinks otherwise: "Why we have set up such environments for new, raw, presumably stressed infants is certainly not obvious. But an outside observer must conclude that the medical profession has decided it doesn't matter to the baby.

"The truth is, it may matter—and a great deal at that. We are not sure yet how much of it matters, although I hope we are on the way toward studies that may determine this. Certainly, many research reports demonstrate how complexly sensitive newborn babies are and how much they can tell us about whether they like or don't like a particular environment. We definitely can no longer assume that they are insensitive lumps, or that treating them as such may not be harmful."[3]

The reports referred to were the product of landmark research by Brazelton, psychologist Lee Salk and others, all of which led to one conclusion: that even at birth the human being possesses remarkable sensory faculties. Far from being "insensitive lumps," newborn babies can see, hear, respond to environmental stimuli, and learn from their responses. In short, each is already a person in his or her own right.

Infants are *particularly* vulnerable, in fact, because their senses lack the organizing filter of developed cortical functions and the background of experience against which new stimuli can be judged. To a baby only hours away from his mother's womb, every change of position, every fluctuation in temperature is new, and therefore unsettling.

Newborn babies do, Brazelton points out, have two very powerful mechanisms for sealing out disturbances in the environment: They can cry or they can go to sleep.

In one study, a bright operating-room light was flashed against a newborn's closed eyes for 20 three-second periods, one minute apart. The first three or four times this was done, the baby exhibited a "startle" response. His heart rate accelerated and then slowed down again; breathing stopped briefly and then resumed at a faster rate. The baby's eyelids also shut more tightly, as though he were trying to ward off the next flashes of light.

By the fourth flash, the infant no longer startled, although his eyes blinked briefly and heart and breathing patterns changed. By the eighth or tenth time, his only response was a blink of the eyelids, and by the fifteenth flash he not only had stopped blinking . . . he had gone to sleep!

"This presumably helpless, insensitive newborn," Brazelton writes, "had *put himself* into a completely effective sleep in which he was no longer at the mercy of cruel researchers such as we."

The baby remained in a sleeping state until three or four minutes after the light was turned off, and then awoke and cried—a justifiable response under the circumstances. What the experiment showed, the researchers concluded, was not only that newborns have the capacity to defend themselves, but also ". . . how assaultive our overlighted environments may be, and how expensive it may well be for an immature organism to use up his physiological resources in this way at the time when he needs them to recover from birth and delivery in order to get going."[4]

Habituation, as this ability to adapt to and finally screen out repetitive stimuli is called, is one of many holdovers from evolutionary inheritance. Quite possibly it was essential to the survival of weak members of the species under adverse environmental conditions. Unfortunately, the response of nervous modern parents to a baby who continuously cries *or* sleeps is far from positive, as later chapters on attachment will make clear.

27

That pain does "hurt" newborn babies has been shown in a number of studies involving observation of increases in infant muscle tension and changes in heart rate and breathing patterns, as well as more obvious signs such as crying. These have confirmed that infants react defensively to high-intensity stimuli (for example, loud noises, abrupt movement, sudden removal of all means of support) and feel discomfort when subjected to unpleasant physical sensations (such as pricking of the infant's heel to obtain a blood sample).

But what about the pain of birth itself? Is the fetus capable of more than simple reflex action? How conscious of sensation is the baby during its perilous journey through the birth canal? Here we are treading on shakier ground.

Intrauterine life. That babies move their limbs in response to touch early in gestation is well documented. Around six weeks, the accidental touch of a hand in the area of its mouth will cause the embryo to open its mouth and turn its head away. A few weeks later, the same stimulus will cause the baby to move its head toward the hand, and perhaps insert a finger in its mouth. This is the beginning of the hand-to-mouth rooting reflex and finger sucking so enjoyed by newborns.

At nine weeks, a touch on the sole of the foot will cause the baby to bend its knee and pull the foot away from the contact. Later in gestation, as the uterine walls begin to press more closely, the fetus moves its legs in primitive walking and crawling motions.

We have no way of knowing for certain whether the human being *in utero* distinguishes such stimuli as pleasant or unpleasant —if, in fact, the baby distinguishes them at all. Smiling and frowning looks have been noted at thirty-three weeks and even earlier, but the emotional content of these expressions is still a matter of guesswork. Rhythmic breathing movements, sighing, and hiccuping have been observed by expectant mothers as well as obstetricians. It is believed that certain fetal chest movements may represent primitive attempts to cry. (In those rare cases in which air accidentally makes its way into a mother's uterus in late pregnancy, true crying noises may be overhead.)

Similarly, little is known about how much the fetus is actually capable of seeing, although the baby makes eye movements very early in gestation in both waking and sleeping states. It is likely

Perhaps, simply by changing the postpartum environment, the baby could be comforted sufficiently to prevent later neurosis?

He began to consider the conditions under which infants are conventionally brought into the world: the harsh lights, unfamiliar noises, sudden stretching of the newborn spine as the wailing infant is dangled by his heels, the abrupt cutting of the previously life-sustaining umbilical cord.

Why, babies cry because they are in agony, he thought, and *Birth Without Violence* was born.

Yes, so few things are essential. None of these costly gadgets for monitoring, none of the other things that are the pride of our technology and are so in fashion now.

None of them.

Only a little patience and humility. A little silence. Unobtrusive but real attention. Awareness of the newcomer as a person. Unselfconsciousness.

And love is necessary too.[7]

In advocating gentle handling of the newborn, it must be pointed out that Leboyer was not operating entirely in a vacuum. The obstetrical tradition of his own native France had already produced the great physicians Fernand Lamaze and Pierre Vellay, whose maternity hospital, the Château Belvedere, was world renowned for considerate care of mothers and newborns. And in other parts of Europe, particularly the Netherlands* and Scandinavia, uncomplicated deliveries had always been carried out under normal lighting conditions and the babies gently placed skin to skin against their mothers for stroking and nursing, without particular fanfare or publicity.

Still, as Sir William Osler once said, "In science the credit goes to the man who convinces the world, not to the man to whom the idea first occurs."[8] And—lionized, disparaged, unquestionably controversial—Frederick Leboyer was clearly a man with an idea whose time had come.

---

* That little nation in recent times has stood at the forefront of both humanity *and* safety in childbearing. With most deliveries attended by midwives or general practitioners, minimal drug usage, and a minuscule cesarean section rate, Dutch infant mortality figures have consistently been the lowest in the world (well beneath those of the United States) thanks to excellent prenatal care, careful screening and close supervision of high-risk pregnancies, and efficient emergency backup services.

NOTES

1. Arthur Janov and E. Michael Holden, *Primal Man: The New Consciousness* (New York: Thomas Y. Crowell, 1975), pp. 83–84.
2. Arthur Janov, *The Primal Scream* (New York: G. P. Putnam's Sons, 1970), p. 88.
3. T. Berry Brazelton, "The Miracle of Birth: How Babies See Their World," *Redbook,* March 1978, p. 112.
4. *Ibid.*
5. Aidan Macfarlane, *The Psychology of Childbirth* (Cambridge, Mass.: Harvard University Press, 1977), p. 56.
6. Lee Salk, "The Need for Humanized Perinatal Care," *Contemporary Ob/Gyn,* April 1977, pp. 110–114.
7. Frederick Leboyer, *Birth Without Violence* (New York: Alfred A. Knopf, 1975), pp. 111–112.
8. William Osler, address, Royal Society of Medicine, May 15, 1918.

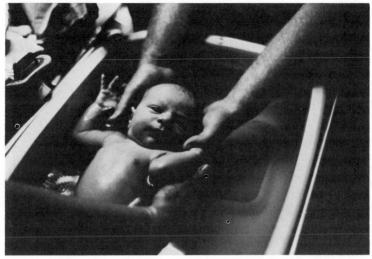

Courtesy of David Kliot, M.D.

3 · Birth Without Violence

What makes being born so frightful is the intensity, the boundless scope and variety of the experience, its suffocating richness.

People say—and believe—that a newborn baby feels nothing. He feels everything.

Everything—utterly, without choice or filter or discrimination.

Frederick Leboyer, Birth Without Violence

The idea behind nonviolent birth was as simple as it was revolutionary. Human beings like the status quo, Leboyer reasoned. If I were a human being about to be born, accustomed only to darkness and rhythmic body sounds, how would it feel to emerge suddenly into a noisy, glaringly bright environment with no softness or vestige of the familiar?

Having as yet no concept of self versus other, expecting the gentle support of amniotic fluid and the tight embrace of the uterine walls, how would I then react to being abruptly separated from my mother and held upside down in midair?

Why (when nature has provided that normal babies begin to breathe without any artificial stimulation) must I be subjected to the pain and indignity of a slap on the feet or buttocks? Why are they thrusting tubes into my nose and mouth and clamping the umbilical cord—my last link with paradise—before it has even stopped pulsating? Why is everyone so glad that I am crying? Can't they see that I am in pain and *I am human, too?*

As clearly as he saw the problem, Leboyer grasped the solution: lessen the trauma. In the first moments of life, welcome the newborn with reassurance and love, rather than silver nitrate drops. "Let us see," he wrote, "how even a modest increase of sensitivity on our part can make an immense difference."[1]

FREE AT LAST

Unlike the embryonic phase, during which the growth of the nurturing sac outstrips that of the child within, the latter part of pregnancy is marked by progressive shrinking of the fetal universe. Where once the child could stretch and move without restraint, supported by the buoyant waters, now the uterine walls close more tightly around it with each passing day. Gradually, the fetus curls up into a ball, preparing for the moment when its world begins to quake and the "prison cell" becomes a narrow tunnel to freedom.

The passage created by the cervix and vagina is barely large enough for a moderate-sized infant presenting normally; breech babies and those whose heads are large with respect to the size of the mother's pelvis find the going even more difficult and treacherous. The force of labor contractions press the fetal head against the passage time and again, until finally a way opens—and the head "crowns." Soft, membrane-covered spaces between the bones of the baby's head, called fontanels, allow for some reshaping or "molding" to take place as the head is delivered. The extent to which a newborn's head may be temporarily flattened during the course of a perfectly normal delivery gives us some idea of the trauma to which the infant has just been exposed.

Having come through the ordeal in safety, how is the baby greeted?

When the infant emerges, the doctor seizes it by one foot and holds it dangling, head down.

As usual, his intentions are good.

The infant's body is, in fact, quite slippery, coated as it is with vernix caseosa, the thick, white grease that covers it from head to toe. The infant is held by the foot to prevent it from slipping and falling. Such a handhold is sure. Convenient.

Convenient for us.

And for the infant?

What does it feel, finding itself suddenly upside down?

Indescribable vertigo.

Those who have had nightmares in which they plunge suddenly into a void are familiar with this sensation. It stems directly from this moment during their birth.[2]

The fragile perceptions of the newborn cannot cope with being dangled in midair, just as, according to the researchers, they cannot cope with overbright lighting or loud noises. All sensation is new, nothing has logic or meaning. The result of this overpowering totality of experience is mindless terror.

To protect newborn babies from this kind of sensory overkill, Leboyer decided to try revealing the world to them in gradual stages, accompanying each stage with reminders of life in the womb. All of his techniques—and he dislikes to call them that, claiming that we are already overscientific and "drowning" in techniques—are aimed at forging "a link between past and present; to ensure that in this totally unknown and seemingly antagonistic universe, some familiar thing is there to reassure and appease."[3]

THE QUIET MIRACLE

If babies could voice their opinions in the matter, how might they wish to be born?

In subdued light, for one thing, and without unnecessary noise.

While it is believed that the fetus *in utero* can hear and see, these sensations must necessarily be muted by the liquid environment of the amniotic sac and the overwhelming presence of the mother —her steady heartbeat, digestive rumblings, and so forth. The baby is totally unprepared for operating-room lighting conditions and the clattering of stainless-steel tables.

Complete darkness and speechlessness are neither necessary nor desirable; the obstetrical team requires sufficient light to observe the condition of the mother-infant pair, and the parents (whose voices are already known to the baby) will naturally want to express their pleasure and congratulate one another. But this can be accomplished with respect for the infant's sensibilities, just as the delivery-room temperature can be adjusted to the comfort level of the lightly draped mother and child.

The umbilical cord should be allowed to finish pulsating before it is severed. As long as the infant is receiving oxygen from this source, there will be no danger of anoxia and no panic on the baby's part as the first sharp rush of air enters the respiratory tree. As the blood vessels leading to and from the placenta are naturally sealed off, the newborn makes the transition to pulmonary breathing with scarcely a murmur.

The practice of routinely clamping the cord from forty-five seconds to one minute after birth is a holdover from the days of general anesthesia, when it really was advisable to "get the baby out" in a hurry. (General anesthesia for delivery diminishes the newborn's ability to breathe, cough, and expel mucus and secretions. With its increasing popularity earlier in the century, removal of the infant from the mother for resuscitation became a matter of course.) Although such active intervention is seldom warranted today, there are specific cases—as when the placenta begins to separate or the cord is wrapped tightly around the baby's neck—in which the cord must be severed as a safety precaution.

Instead of suspending the baby upside down by his ankles, which jerks the fragile spine and terrifies the infant, the attendants should gently raise the baby onto his mother's exposed abdomen and place him face down in a "postural drainage" position. Little or no suction is generally needed; the baby's fluids will be absorbed naturally without interference.

Thus, while the cord continues to beat, mother and child are allowed a few minutes of quiet recovery time. Protected from

ambient room temperatures by the warmth of her body
sured by the soft pressure of her hands and the comforting
of her heartbeat, the newborn gains the confidence to slowly un
curl his own body, limb by limb.

Through her hands that do not move, yet are charged with tenderness, the mother is saying to her baby:
"Don't be afraid; I'm here. We're both safe, you and I; we're both
alive."[4]

Once the cord has stopped pulsating, it can be clamped and
tied. In traditional deliveries, this would be the moment for
the baby to be weighed, for silver nitrate drops to be squeezed
into the tightly closed eyes, and for the routine pediatric assessment.

"Wait," advises Leboyer. All of these things can be done just as
well in half an hour. The cold steel of the scale, the sting of the
unfamiliar drops, all the prying and poking and measuring will
only aggravate the child. Instead, place the infant in an environment he can understand and love—place him in water!

In the weightlessness of a bath which has been heated to body
temperature, the little figure at last relaxes completely. The baby
opens his eyes and calmly observes his environment. He gazes
first at one parent, then at the other. As for the body:

Movement, now, is everything.
The head turns—to the right, to the left—slowly, twisting around as
far as the neck will allow.
The face is in perfect profile.
A hand stirs—opens, closes—and emerges from the water. The arm
follows, rising. The hand caresses the sky, feels the space around it, falls
again.
The other hand rises in its turn, traces an arabesque, and then, in its
turn, descends.
Now they play together, meet, embrace, separate.
One moves away, the other darts after it.
One pauses, dreams, opens and closes with the slowness of the sea.
The other falls under the same spell. The two dreams mirror each other:
hands like flowers about to blossom. Sea anemones, they breathe with
the slow cradling rhythm of the world beneath the ocean, moved by its
invisible currents . . .
The child is playing!

37

And not ten minutes have gone by since it was born!

This entire ballet is taking place in profound silence, punctuated only by soft little cries—exclamations of surprise and joy.

Sometimes solemn, sometimes playful, completely absorbed in its discoveries, the child explores, tests the space inside, outside, around it with a concentration that never falters, that never succumbs to distractions.

Totally *there*, an impassioned observer of its own body.[5]

Having been slowly lifted from the water, dried, dressed, and returned to his mother for suckling, the infant's journey is ended at last. Quiet and alert, rather than fearful, the baby is ready for the medical routines which have been postponed—not for an hour or two, but for a few minutes only—on his behalf. Enough time to still the cries, calm the thrashing limbs and uncurl the tiny fists.

"There are no ugly babies," Leboyer writes. "Only those deformed by fear."[6]

THE CRITICS SPEAK

Leboyer anticipated that his ideas would meet with a cold reception from the bulk of the medical community. The very concept of inaction, of quiet observation of the baby's condition rather than outright intervention, he knew would be incomprehensible to many of his colleagues. "I am not criticizing doctors," he told one interviewer. "They are really doing their best, and they are sincerely feeling that they are doing their best, no doubt. The physical aspect of things has to be tackled. The needs of the body are to be looked at very, very carefully. My only point is that in birth, the requirements of the body are one thing, but the emotional aspect is just as important and has been completely neglected."[7]

To those who accused him of denying the progress of obstetrics, he replied that he approved of scientific advancement and was glad to make use of up-to-date equipment—where it was needed to ensure safety. His argument was with the coldness and depersonalization of hospital birth as it applied to the healthy newborn, not to the baby at risk.

Whenever breathing appears threatened or the baby responds abnormally in any way, go ahead and put on the lights, cut the cord, use suction, he told physicians. Do whatever must be done. Only think of the consequences *before* applying intensive care procedures to perfectly normal infants; the cost in psychic trauma may far outweigh any need felt by the obstetrician and nursing staff to "do something."

Opponents of the birth-trauma concept have also been vocal in their doubt that altering the quality of the first hour of life can have any real influence on the course of the next ten, twenty, or even fifty years. Leboyer counters that although many factors may affect the development of personality, not all moments in a lifetime have equal significance. Because of the newborn's particular vulnerability, impressions gained during the immediate postpartum period cannot help but be deeply imbedded in the psyche. If by a few simple routines these initial impressions can be made actually positive, rather than threatening, should we not consider this simply preventive medicine?

Finally, Leboyer reminded critics who complained about the distinctively unscientific tone of the book itself that childbirth was also passion, and the problem was exactly that the ecstasy had been removed and replaced by medical interventions! Each birth has within itself the potential of being a "nativity," he insisted, uplifting all who take part or even witness it.

The cult of suffering. Behind much of the resistance to gentleness in childbirth has been reluctance to abandon the old assumption that "suffering builds character." But what does a difficult birth actually teach? In all probability, it teaches the lesson that existence is a ceaseless struggle, in which one must act as the aggressor simply in order to survive.

Is this the sort of legacy we wish to impart to infants less than an hour old?

Birth without violence breeds children who are strong because they are free, without conflict. Free and fully awake.

Aggression is not strength, it is exactly the opposite.

Aggression and violence are the masks of weakness, impotence, and fear.

Strength is sure, sovereign, smiling.[8]

THE GENTLE BIRTH BOOK

Nowhere in obstetrics, says Leboyer, has the cult of suffering been more clearly demonstrated than in the classic attitude toward the newborn's first cries. Supposedly, the baby is slapped to stimulate it to breathe, although this is hardly ever necessary with unmedicated childbirth and only occasionally with epidural or local anesthesia. Naturally, the baby wails, and physician and parents heave a sigh of relief:

> The reflexes are normal. The machine works. But are we machines?
> Aren't cries always an expression of pain?
> Isn't it conceivable that the baby is in anguish?
> What makes us assume that birth is less painful for the child than it is for the mother?[9]

Newborn infants cannot verbalize their pain, but they *can* call attention to its existence. As the young primate's cry in the wild alerts its mother to the approach of a predator, modern man in his infancy continues to express his isolation, his fear.

Yes, Leboyer agrees, the infant may need to cry out once, or perhaps twice, to give evidence that his breathing is not obstructed. But that is all. There should be no wailing, no heartbreaking sobs.

As for the proponents of the hard line:

> These are the same people who used to say (or who even now still say): "Women suffer in childbirth. All right, that must be because they have to" . . .
> This kind of suffering is without point. It serves no purpose. It satisfies no God. It springs from a failure of intelligence.
> Natural childbirth—childbirth without pain—stands as proof of this.[10]

The analogy to natural childbirth is apt. In attempting to do for the newborn what his French colleagues had already done for expectant mothers, Leboyer made no claims that his method was infallible—only that it was better. Lamaze and Vellay had always insisted that because of individual variations in pelvic structure, degree of family support, and so forth, not every woman would be able to have a joyous, pain-free childbirth. Similarly, Leboyer reminds us each baby is a completely unique individual. We cannot expect that every one will awake to life peacefully.

Each baby travels this path in its own manner . . .

Some babies seem to bound into life, then suddenly withdraw into their own anger.

Others go on struggling, eyes tight shut, incapable of realizing that their ordeal is over, that they have been born. It is immensely difficult wresting them from their nightmares, from their fears.

Others emerge casually, barely utter a cry, open their eyes, and begin to play! [11]

But we can try. We can help the placid babies retain their centeredness by avoiding unnecessary interventions (which in some cases seem designed precisely to *make* them cry), and we can soothe the agitated babies by replacing our excessively stimulating environments with settings more reminiscent of intrauterine life.

"But these ideas are very new; there are hardly any data to support them as yet," say the traditionalists.

True enough—although there undoubtedly will be more in the near future. But science is often very unscientific. Many accepted practices in medicine are based, not on mathematical calculation, but on the simple premise that they work. It is not always necessary to understand the mechanisms behind a new therapy in order to practice it effectively.

We do not, for example, know exactly how Lamaze techniques cause reduction in the number of pain sensations felt by the laboring mother, yet it is undeniable that they suceed in doing so in many, many cases. It should be enough for the critics that gentle birthing can—with minimal changes in ordinary hospital routine, no lessening of safety, and willing cooperation on the part of the new parents (who are only too eager to cuddle and hold their baby)—transform what may be a long and difficult struggle in which everyone is left feeling exhausted and emotionally drained into something elevating and beautiful.

NOTES

1. Frederick Leboyer, *Birth Without Violence* (New York: Alfred A. Knopf, 1975), p. 35.
2. Ibid., p. 21.
3. Ibid., p. 102.

4. Ibid., p. 72.
5. Ibid., pp. 84–90.
6. Ibid., p. 108.
7. Michael Toms, "Birth Without Violence: An Interview with Dr. Frederick Leboyer," *New Age Journal,* October 1975, p. 21.
8. Leboyer, *Birth Without Violence,* p. 110.
9. Ibid., p. 5.
10. Ibid., p. 111.
11. Ibid., p. 107.

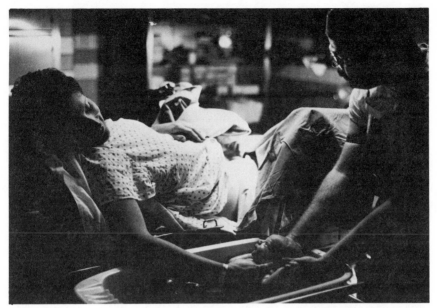

Courtesy of David Kliot, M.D.

4 · Gentle Birth: The American Experience

There really was a sensational change in the atmosphere of the delivery room when the lights were turned down. We are all so accustomed to "lights, camera, action," to the swinging electrical doors, intercoms going off, basins clanging . . . it's hard to imagine how much noise there is until it stops. With all the commotion, all the instrumentation, the emotional content of the moment for the woman and her husband could be virtually ignored. As soon as the lights were dimmed, however, all eyes were automatically directed toward the birthing process.

David Kliot, M.D.

Despite the fanfare that accompanied Leboyer's American tour, few physicians in the United States and Canada chose to follow his example in their own practices. As noted already, our medical establishment is generally lukewarm, if not downright hostile, in its attitude toward reformers. Advocates of nonviolence did not delude themselves; it would be a slow, uphill struggle convincing their colleagues to change tactics.

For those open-minded enough to try, however, there was no going back. "When I think of how casually I used to pick up babies and slap them," one obstetrician told me, "I shudder." In small—but ever-increasing—numbers, physicians and midwives across the continent began offering their maternity patients the option of "quiet" birth. And as the readership of *Birth Without Violence* grew, informed expectant mothers began to request, even demand, that approach for themselves.

Among the pioneers of nonviolent childbirth in the United States, the names of obstetricians John W. Grover and David Kliot are outstanding. Instinctively sensing that Leboyer's assumptions about newborn suffering were correct, these physicians set about proving the safety of his techniques, modifying them slightly in the direction of family-centered care, and incorporating them into their standard obstetrical management. Amazed at the responsiveness of the babies and the depth of feeling displayed by the parents, they then began the task of persuading the hospitals with which they were associated to consider offering gentle birth to all women in labor except those with serious medical complications.

As we follow the course of gentle childbirth on this side of the Atlantic, readers' will soon notice that there has been a major philosophical shift—from "baby-centered" to "family-centered." Whereas Leboyer himself was overwhelmingly concerned with the infant's responses (even, at times, to the exclusion of the mother . . . certainly to the exclusion of the father), the Americans who have adopted these methods see the parents' role as integral to shaping the kind of person that child will become.

By creating a setting in which both parents assist in the delivery and are themselves responsible for the immediate care of the newborn, these practitioners feel they are laying the groundwork for development of close emotional bonds between mother, father, and baby.

"Personally, I doubt that a single isolated experience in a child's life is *quite* as important as Leboyer tells us," Grover notes. "I really believe that what we're doing is creating caring parents who are able to provide a nurturing environment for the child. We have only to look at what happens when parents are deprived of a positive early contact experience to reach our own conclusions about the importance of such early communication."

REBEL AT HARVARD

As a young obstetrical resident, John Grover recalls being horrified by the bizarre effects of the so-called twilight sleep on laboring patients. Considered a humane approach to childbearing, this drug-induced amnesia regularly transformed healthy pregnant women into restless, incoherent sleepwalkers or shrieking maniacs who literally had to be strapped down for their own safety.

With the growth of interest in natural childbirth in the mid-1960s, Grover became an enthusiastic advocate of preparation and verbal support to replace drugs in labor. "My patients were looking for a more satisfying childbirth experience," he explains. "They wanted to both witness and participate in the miracle of birth. And who could blame them?"

Physically prepared, educated for the task at hand, and free of the fear and confusion that had troubled generations of her predecessors, the Lamaze-prepared mother was clearly a species apart from the traditional obstetrical patient.

But it soon became apparent that there were still pieces missing from the puzzle. Where, for example, was the baby's father?

"We realized," says Grover, "that here was a family being born, and yet fathers were still being asked to wait outside while their wives labored in isolation or attended by strangers. No wonder they felt agitated and left out of hospital births and afraid to pick up their babies once they got home!"

The campaign to allow fathers into the delivery room alongside their wives—a logical outgrowth of the natural childbirth movement—was conducted on a nationwide scale. Aided by feminist activism and the undeniable fact that there just weren't enough trained labor monitrices, or "coaches," around to handle all of the women who wanted an unmedicated childbirth experience, willing fathers were able to gain access to delivery rooms for normal and, in many instances, even nonemergency cesarean births.

With drug usage reduced (or at least under better control) and the partnership of both parents in delivery finally accepted, the reformers turned their attention to the surroundings in which birth takes place at most hospital centers. Why, they demanded to know, are perfectly healthy mothers and babies commonly subjected to intensive care interventions? What effect might such standard practices as routine surgical prepping, withholding of food, electronic fetal monitoring, and use of the operating room for delivery have on the morale of apprehensive parents-to-be? Is there a relation between the familiar condition known as "postpartum blues" and the new mother's disappointment at being abruptly separated from her baby and then seeing him only at the convenience of nursery personnel? What influence might such a regimented schedule have on the early success or failure of breast feeding? And why, when women in primitive societies seem to encounter no problems getting their babies to nurse, do educated American women find the task so difficult, even overwhelming?

It was into this charged atmosphere of questioning of accepted medical procedures—and the establishment of various childbirth alternatives, both in and out of hospital—that *Birth Without Violence* made its American debut.

The concept of a nonviolent birth seemed to Grover to be directly linked to all of the other humanistic innovations. Although at the time he had serious reservations about certain of Leboyer's ideas (the wisdom of the bath, in particular), he did go so far as to reexamine his own delivery-room techniques, such as holding the baby upside down and·stimulating it to elicit a cry.

"It was rather an unpleasant shock," he recalls, "to find that I had been repeating these rituals, not out of conviction that they were medically advisable, but simply because *this was the manner in which I had been taught* to deliver babies."

Grover's first meeting with Leboyer, in that spring of 1975, proved decisive. "I perceived clearly then that our motives and goals were the same," he recollects. "Both of us hoped to provide a more positive human experience for everyone. The only difference was that I approached the task from the perspective of the parents, and he from the perspective of the infant."

A few weeks afterward, with considerable nervousness but unprecedented support from his delivery-room staff, John Grover became the first physician in the Boston area to undertake a family-centered Leboyer delivery: "I noticed immediately that babies born in this peaceful, twilight atmosphere seemed calmer and more alert than those I had delivered in the past. After a while the nursery nurses began to comment, 'Ah,' you've brought us another gentle birth baby!' without my having to point out the fact. When I asked them how they could tell, the reply was, 'Oh, most babies are either asleep or crying most of the time; yours look about more, they seem to follow us with their eyes.' "

The parental response, says Grover, has been "nothing short of astonishing." Mothers consistently reported feeling more positive about their gently delivered babies than about older siblings at comparable stages of development. As for the fathers, "they seemed more comfortable taking care of the baby, more eager to help, and much more enthusiastic in general than the new fathers we used to encounter." Several women in Grover's practice complained that their husbands tended to monopolize cuddling and caretaking activities to a frustrating degree!

"Having eyes, they see not." At first, Grover worried about his ability to spot unexpected complications without the aid of intense operating-room light. However, he soon learned that the human eye dark-adapts to a surprising degree. Even with the spotlights turned off and only indirect light shining on the perineum, he discovered he had no difficulty performing an episiotomy or using forceps when necessary, judging newborn muscle tone and skin color, or assigning an Apgar score.*

Furthermore, just as the blind often become more accurate observers of detail than the sighted, he found that certain anomalies which tend to be missed at conventional deliveries show up more clearly during gentle birth, as the physician's observation and sense of touch become increasingly acute.

This unexpected benefit was dramatically revealed in a case involving a newborn with a diaphragmatic hernia (life-threatening because it interferes with respiration after birth). The problem was detected within minutes and the baby transferred to the nearby Children's Hospital Medical Center for emergency sur-

* The Apgar score evaluates newborn heart rate, reflexes, muscle tone, respiratory effort, and skin color.

gery. Grover was praised for the unusual speed with which he had identified the abnormality, causing the obstetrician to reflect on "... how easy it is—in the nervous haste of a typical well-lighted hospital birth—for the physician to take a quick look, assume that everything is normal, and turn the infant over to a nurse for observation. It's like the line in the Bible that says: 'Having eyes to see, they see not.' "

One could, I suppose, be nostalgic and recall at this point that babies were once delivered by candlelight or kerosene lamp every night of the week. But instead (with apologies to M. Leboyer) let's take a quick look at the statistics. In several thousand nonviolent deliveries that have already taken place in the United States, *there has not been a single substantiated report of maternal or fetal complications arising from use of gentle birth techniques.* Not one. Nothing but healthy babies, elated parents, and eloquent photographs that speak for themselves.

INVESTIGATOR OF NEWBORN HEART RATES

Although his early championship of prepared, unmedicated childbirth was well known among colleagues and students at Brookdale Hospital and the State University of New York Downstate Medical Center, David Kliot admits that he never would have attempted his first Leboyer delivery had a patient not talked him into it. Today, unless forced by emergency medical considerations, he wouldn't think of doing anything else.

"When I finally read the book," he says, "and reflected on the ideas with my associate, Max Lilling, we realized that there appeared to be at least reasonable substance behind most of them." *Birth Without Violence* gave Kliot and Lilling the incentive they needed to review the medical literature concerning early cord clamping, holding the baby upside down to drain mucus, and the other routines Leboyer objected to so strenuously.

What the literature revealed, they found, was that there was almost no data to support many of the procedures carried out in hospital births and—in sharp contrast to the considerable amount known about the intrauterine environment during pregnancy and labor—very little objective information concerning the delivery period itself. During this most vulnerable time in the life of a human being, when the first gasps of oxygen are drawn and existence hangs by a thread, monitoring was generally discontinued; as a result, little was known about the baby's heart rate at birth and reliance was placed, instead, on such subjective (and potentially misleading) signs as skin color.

Kliot and Lilling were astounded. The birthing of babies in a darkened environment was being condemned by doctors who themselves had only shaky indicators for judging newborn medical status! It appeared that it was not the French physician, but his opponents, who were "in the dark." Comments Kliot: "Infants were being delivered, sometimes with great difficulty involving use of forceps, aspirated, stimulated to make them cry, weighed and measured like so much produce, and given an Apgar score based on *what they looked like,* in contrast to the way we assumed they ought to behave. And nobody (with the obvious exception of Leboyer himself) had ever stopped to think that these procedures —many of which might not even be required and which would certainly appear demeaning if applied to an adult—might in *themselves* be stressful to newborns."

The physicians decided to test Leboyer's hypothesis for themselves. They would do a nonviolent delivery, but maintain a close watch on the baby throughout by means of continuous heart-rate monitoring. Because of the controversial nature of the birth, they selected an early-morning hour, when the hospital was at its most peaceful, to tell the delivery-room nurse: "Turn out the overhead lights and shut the door."

At approximately 3:00 A.M. on the morning of May 15, 1975, baby Elyse came into the world without a cry. Cord still intact, she was placed face down, head to one side, against her mother's abdomen. At approximately twenty seconds after birth, the heart rate was judged satisfactory; a few seconds later, as the spectators watched in tense silence, the newborn infant calmly opened her eyes, lifted her head, and saw her mother for the first time.

"We felt like cheering," Kliot remembers. "It was an extraordinary moment."

Word of the experiment soon leaked out among the patients and staff at Brookdale. On the strength of its success and their own solid reputations as clinicians, Kliot and Lilling received de-

partmental permission to develop a study, reviewed by the hospital research committee, of one hundred informed pregnant
women, who were divided into three groups: twenty-five had
standard hospital deliveries; for the remaining seventy-five
women, the lights were dimmed and the baby placed skin to skin
on the mother's abdomen immediately after birth. In the latter
group, the umbilical cords of thirty-seven infants were clamped
immediately, while thirty-eight infants were allowed to remain
attached to their mothers for an additional ten minutes.

The results were, as might be expected, convincing. When the
three groups were compared, the temperatures of the babies left
on their mothers' abdomens were just as high as those of the
control infants warmed under a radiant heater. In the prone position, nasopharyngotracheal drainage occurred without suction;
there was no dangerous inhalation of fluids. All infants' hemato-
crits were normal regardless of the time of cord clamping, and
there was no increase in bilirubinemia, as had been feared earlier.

The newborn heart rate, easily monitored by hand and stethoscope, proved to be a very accurate indicator of oxygen status. (In
later nonviolent deliveries, the investigators were able to detect
respiratory problems by the mere failure of the heart rate to *speed
up* immediately following birth, as they found would normally be
the case.)

And of course there was an undeniable change in the responsiveness of mother, father, and baby, when given the opportunity
to exchange their first greetings in comparative privacy. "All
women regard the process of labor and delivery somewhat differ-
ently," notes Kliot, "but we found by and large that not only were
the infants more relaxed and alert, but the mothers liked the
peace and privacy of the darkened delivery room as much as the
babies did."

After ascertaining the safety of these aspects of the Leboyer
approach, Kliot and Lilling added the warm-water bath to their
newborn management. At last the fathers had something to do,
besides merely sitting at their wives' bedside. No longer passive
observers, they were in direct tactile and visual contact with their
infants, and the results showed up almost immediately.

"There has been a notable difference in the number of men
who accompany their wives at the postpartum visit," Kliot points
out: ". . . instead of leaving the baby at home with a sitter, in many

cases the entire family comes in as a group, and the father holds the infant while the mother is examined.

"And there *is* a difference in the babies. At least, the mothers tell us there is. I get fewer reports of colic, poor feeding, incessant crying, and all the other things that generally aggravate new mothers. Whether this is just a reflection of the mothers' own positive birth experience, or whether the babies themselves are actually calmer, remains to be shown. But I think we can say with certainty that the interrelationship has been affected, and in a very positive way."

Other studies indicate that gentle birth babies are, in fact, calmer. In one experiment in Florida, twenty infants delivered by modified Leboyer methods were compared to seventeen controls used a standard index of newborn behavior patterns. Babies in the control group, the investigators noted, ". . . tended to exhibit body tension, blink, cry, suck, and tremble or shudder more than neonates [newborns] in the experimental group. Newborns in the experimental group tended to exhibit body relaxation, open their eyes, and grunt, sigh, or make other soft sounds more than newborns in the control group. Behaviors characteristic of the experimental group were especially noted when the infant was in the water bath; he typically demonstrated a slackening of the muscles, open eyes, lack of crying, and exploratory movements."[1]

As in the deliveries supervised by Drs. Grover, Kliot, and Lilling, "no complications occurred in mothers or infants which could be attributed to the gentle birth method."[2] Rectal temperatures were completely satisfactory. No tendency toward infant anemia was observed, and of the six cases of physiologic jaundice, four occurred in the controls and only two in the experimental group.

"Results of this study," the experimenters concluded, "indicate the Leboyer method is safe for mother and infant and promotes infant relaxation in the delivery room."[3]

IS GENTLE BIRTH FOR ME?

Kliot and Lilling have already performed over fifteen hundred nonviolent deliveries at Brookdale Hospital, routinely using Leboyer techniques not only in normal spontaneous and low-forceps births but in breech, cesarean, and uncomplicated premature deliveries as well.*

However, we must emphasize that every institution has its own protocols concerning medical practice in labor and delivery. Although the rules are occasionally bent (as happened in the case of baby Elyse) and may be regularly amended to incorporate new developments in obstetrical and newborn care, it's always better to avoid unpleasant last-minute surprises.

Therefore, if you are beginning to think in terms of a family-centered gentle childbirth experience, it's best to begin from the premise that you may have to (1) do some comparison shopping well in advance, or (2) be extremely persuasive and tactful in making your wishes known to those in charge of delivering and caring for your baby.

What if there are complications? True emergency situations are fortunately infrequent in obstetrics; when they occur, concern for the safety of mother and child must naturally override all other considerations. The decision to proceed with a gentle birth ultimately depends upon the medical status of mother and fetus at the time of delivery.

Certain specific situations, such as emergency cesarean section requiring general anesthesia, may preclude the Leboyer approach; however, routine cesarean section with a spinal anesthetic need not prevent a couple from enjoying this initial extra contact. Although bright lights are obviously needed for the operative procedure, the physician can shield the baby's eyes with his hand and then, after checking his condition, turn him over to his father for cuddling while the incision is being closed. After that, it's bathtime, again the father's responsibility (just as it would be in a pelvic delivery), but the tub is placed close enough to the mother so that she, too, can watch and talk softly to the infant as he is being bathed.

In other cases, as when pregnancy and birth are complicated by hypertensive disease or diabetes in the mother, low birth weight,

---

* It might even be suggested that the calming effect on both baby and parents of the subdued light, lowered voices, and slower pace of gentle birth is particularly well-suited to countering the tension that inevitably develops when a degree of medical intervention is called for. Similarly, the increased opportunity for parental-infant contact seems highly desirable in those situations where a longer recuperative period, possibly involving separation of mother and infant, is needed, in view of the fact that these are the very settings in which later parenting problems may be anticipated.

meconium staining, or any of a number of other relatively common problems, certain procedures may be abbreviated or eliminated and a pediatrician or neonatologist (physician specializing in newborn management) asked to attend.

It is important to keep in mind that gentle birth is an *approach* —an attitude, really—rather than a rigid format. Leboyer repeatedly insisted that his methods required little in the way of preparation. Indeed, they are flexible enough to be instituted or withdrawn literally at a moment's notice. "The key," says John Grover, "is adaptability; fostering a warm, sensitive environment, yet remaining in a position to immediately respond, should a threatening situation develop."

If injection of medication is called for at any time during the course of delivery, the lights are easily turned up for that procedure and then adjusted downward again, or not, as appropriate. Should a presumably healthy infant suddenly go into laryngospasm and require resuscitation, emergency measures can be begun at once—provided the birth is taking place in a hospital where such equipment is available.

Gentle childbirth does not disregard technology; it merely puts it in its appropriate place. The fact is that in the vast majority of pregnancies, aggressive management of the newborn is neither necessary nor desirable. So let's take a look at a more typical situation, and see what actually happens during that crucial hour or so in which . . .

A CHILD IS BORN

"O.K., it's time to push," says the obstetrician.

At first, you don't believe it. Nine months of waiting, of reading, of attending childbirth education class . . . watching the hours tick by during the irregular contractions of first-stage labor . . . more waiting . . . then panting and blowing like mad to overcome the discomfort of transition . . . all in preparation for this moment.

Mother and father wash their hands with ordinary soap and water. He dons a scrub suit, then helps adjust the pillows at the head of the delivery bed, which has already been tilted up about 45 degrees. She stares down at the immense surface of her abdomen, now gaily tinted "antiseptic orange." Then the lights are dimmed and voices in the room are stilled, waiting. . . .

"Push," the delivery-room nurse whispers close to her ear. "Push."

The baby's head and shoulders emerge. "Would you like to help?" asks the obstetrician. Gratefully, the mother nods between pushes. Reaching down, she grasps her baby as the doctor gently pulls him up and places him face down onto the bare skin of her belly.

When the mother is allowed to complete the delivery herself in this way, she feels an enormous sense of relief. "It's as though," Grover says, "a psychological link is forged between the fetus she has carried for nine months and the warm and wet infant resting snugly against her body." Not only does this simple act prevent the onset of an "empty womb" syndrome, but many parents have described it as the most meaningful moment in the entire delivery.

If the infant's mouth is filled with mucus this is gently suctioned; most babies, however, cough vigorously and clear their throats by themselves. Mother and father slowly massage the baby as they have been taught to do in their prenatal classes, and call him by name for the first time. They are not concerned if he cries only once or twice, in surprise at beginning to breathe, or even if he doesn't cry at all. For this, too, they have been prepared. Notes Grover: "I warn all of my couples in advance that there is nothing positive about a loud cry. It is a sign of panic or fear or pain, which we in our ignorance have come to regard as normal. At one time, it was commonplace for infants to cry for five minutes or more before settling down. Now approximately half whimper for 30 seconds or so, while the rest only cough or grunt and begin to look around with interest. It is not the babies who have changed, but our techniques of handling them which have made all the difference."

Babies were routinely picked up by the ankles, spanked, or otherwise stimulated to cry in order to test their reflexes for the one- and five-minute Apgar scores. The logic was irrefutable: An agitated baby—muscles tensed, "yelling its lungs out" in protest —was obviously breathing! The fact is that by careful monitoring of the heart rate, respiration, cord pulse, muscle tone, and coordinated behavior in the first minutes after birth, the same evaluation can be performed without disturbing baby or parents in the slightest.

And, Kliot suggests, probably with greater medical accuracy, as well: "It doesn't take enormous electrical wattage or a loud cry to tell you that a baby is not in respiratory distress. Yet the complete ritual continues to be observed, in spite of its dehumanizing effect and the lack of supportive evidence. For such is the power of ritual . . ."

Still connected to his mother's body by the pulsating umbilical cord, protected from cold stress by her warmth on one side and a light blanket on the other, our baby now has a chance to discover his surroundings at his own pace. In the dim light, his eyes open and, glancing around, rest at first briefly and then for longer intervals on those of his parents. If someone in the room speaks, the baby's gaze will shift in the speaker's direction; if the proud father photographs the moment, the alert ears react to the sound at once.

"He's got your father's nose," whispers the mother, and both parents laugh softly. The tone of their conversation is intimate, and in fact the medical personnel, hidden in the shadows, seem far removed from the proceedings. It is the baby who completely captures their attention, and by his incredible responsiveness to their look, their voices, and, above all, their touch, he does not disappoint them.

"Labor," cautions Grover, "provides many opportunities for eager new mothers and fathers to feel that they have failed in some way. If the mother needed medication, or even if she didn't —but yelled or cried or forgot what she learned in class—or if her husband wasn't properly supportive, there is a tendency on the part of the parents to feel that they haven't really done a good job." Whereas gentle childbirth is almost "failure-proof." With hardly any effort at all on their part, simply by allowing the infant to show off what he can do, the parents gain a sense of accomplishment. Grover says, "When that baby looks at his mother and father and appears to perceive them intelligently, their immediate, instinctual response is to tell themselves: 'We've done well.' "

In a traditional delivery, the cord would have been cut immediately after birth and the baby whisked away for weighing and measuring. But weight and measurement do not change appreciably during the first hour of life; why perform these interventions now, when the infant is content to be beside his mother?

As for temperature, this is maintained by the skin-to-skin contact and further ensured by lightly covering both mother and baby. In repeated temperature comparisons, Grover, Kliot, and other investigators found no evidence that the Leboyer babies' temperatures were significantly different from those of other babies admitted to their respective nurseries on the same day. (In fact, they were generally higher.)

Nature, as always, has provided marvelously well for her own. To a newborn needing comfort, no infant warmer has the look, smell, and texture of his mother's body. And the very knowledge that she is capable of shielding her child from harm gives an incredible boost to the new mother's ego.

By about seven minutes after delivery, the pulsations of the umbilical cord have ceased. The cord is then clamped and divided. Now the baby is ready for his bath! Gingerly, his father lifts him into the little tub;* if the placenta has already been delivered, mother helps, too. The infant may startle and cry briefly at first being separated from her, but the touch of the water is almost instantly soothing. At first his movements are hesitant and jerky . . . his body has been confined for so long . . . but with a little reassurance from the hands that encompass him, he soon learns to move his limbs about in long, graceful arcs.

"Look, he's swimming!" cries the mother, delighted. And, in fact, that is exactly what the baby is doing. This is an environment he knows and understands; in the weightlessness of the water, he again feels at home.

Observers have noted that the babies seem most alert at this stage. Certainly, there is a great deal of eye contact and verbal give-and-take between infant and parents. About one in ten newborns, by Grover's count, actually seem to smile with contentment, as seen in Leboyer's original photographs. That a bath may be simultaneously relaxing and mildly stimulating to an infant should hardly come as a surprise to any adult who has ever splashed water on his face to "wake up" in the morning, or sunk appreciatively into a warm tub after a grueling day at work!

After five to ten minutes in the tub, the baby is gently removed

---

* When modified Leboyer deliveries were first attempted in the United States, strict surgical precautions were observed, including use of sterilizable stainless-steel basins and costly sterile water for bathing. Today, the fear of infection has been dispelled, and procedures are more relaxed. A clean plastic Bathinette filled with warm tap water is considered perfectly acceptable. Baby is more comfortable and, besides, it's a nice way of introducing the parents to what will, in very short order, become an everyday ritual.

to a warmed treatment table where he is dried thoroughly, identified, and given prophylactic eye treatment. Rectal temperature is checked, and then the infant, wrapped in a warm blanket, is given to his mother for suckling.

Everything is done in a slow, relaxed manner; there is no need to rush. And again, the mother has grounds for confidence: Because her baby has had plenty of time to recover from the shock of being born, he will take to the breast much more quickly and nurse with more concentration than would otherwise have been the case.*

In placing the baby at her breast, the mother moves a step further in the process of nurturing that had its roots in pregnancy and was first realized when she helped ease him out of the birth canal and onto her belly. The warmth of the tiny body, its overwhelming need to be held and caressed, its craving for her milk, the certain knowledge that this baby is *hers* . . . all evoke feelings of tenderness and protectiveness that are almost indescribable.

As for the baby, he is learning to trust in his environment and, already, in the ability of his own actions to provoke a sympathetic response. While the actual effect of gentle birthing on the registering of first-line traumas is merely speculative, this much is already clear: It establishes a climate for parental-infant interaction that is very difficult, if not actually impossible, to duplicate under ordinary hospital conditions. During every moment of this crucial early period in which he is so responsive, our baby is learning a lesson about security, about what it feels like to be held and loved, that later experience will be hard-pressed to match.

And all with only slight changes in standard delivery-room practices, no additional cost in terms of equipment or staff, and only a few extra minutes of the physician's time!

For, as the baby (now about fifteen minutes old) quietly nurses or snuggles against his mother once again, the lights are already gradually beginning to pick up. Soon the process of adaptation to ordinary room light and sound will conclude with the family

---

* When I was a brand-new mother, my pediatrician, who strongly encouraged breast feeding, warned me repeatedly not to expect my baby to nurse well from the start. The fact that suckling did not come naturally to mothers—or babies—was an unnerving thought and reflected the still-prevalent belief that breast feeding was fraught with difficulties for Western mothers. *And so*—with our babies either crying incessantly or drugged into oblivion, sugar-water supplementation in the hospital nursery, and a case of formula in our take-home "goody bag"—*it was!*

being transferred to the recovery room,* where they can confer with the obstetrician and relive the experience from one another's view. This is the time for discussing what happened in labor and delivery, why the baby did or didn't cry, and what the various observations suggest. It is also a period in which, simply by remaining together as a unit, the family's developing emotional bonds become that much stronger.

Togetherness continues on the postpartum floor, where mother and father jointly learn to care for the baby and exercise their parenting skills in preparation for going home. "The sharing of the work and joys of birth," says Grover, "becomes a peak emotional experience for the family that launches them satisfactorily and positively on the next phase of their journey through life."

T. Berry Brazelton, whose newborn assessment scale has become a standard testing tool in hospitals throughout the country, puts it another way: "I think the main benefit of the Leboyer technique is in the direction of changing the pathological model of delivery into a positive, nurturing one for mother, father and baby. By so doing, we give them all a feeling of importance to each other . . . This is critical if we want to foster parenting and caring about their new babies in a stressful society which almost tears them away from their infants."

Fostering attachment bonds. The physicians who followed Leboyer and modified his delivery practices have placed great stress upon the ability of gentle birth to foster bonding—that process of reciprocal attachment between parents and babies that deepens naturally in the days and weeks after birth, unless some divisive force intervenes to prevent it.

Investigative interest in attachment is a relatively new phenomenon, one that has created great excitement in medicine because of its broad implications for the emotional health of future generations.

It is clear that the mechanisms by which parents come to know and love their children, and vice versa, are not resolved overnight. Rather, there is a subtle progression of involvement that begins

---

* If a "birthing room" is used, this may function as labor, delivery, and recovery room all rolled into one.

even before the child's birth and continues (in all probability) until the young man or woman reaches adulthood.

Every experience encountered along this route, whether mundane or catastrophic, will exert some influence on the outcome. But there can be little doubt that it is the earliest experiences— even, as we shall see, those that take place during the first hour after birth—that bend the twig from which the mature tree grows.

In order to understand how events in the immediate postpartum period may enhance—or retard—the development of attachment bonds, let us first take a look at how newborns have been programmed, with miraculous precision, to respond to their parents.

NOTES

1. Charlotte M. Oliver and George M. Oliver, "Gentle Birth: Its Safety and Its Effect on Neonatal Behavior," *Journal of Obstetric, Gynecologic and Neonatal Nursing,* September/October 1978, p. 39.
2. Ibid., p. 38.
3. Ibid., p. 35.

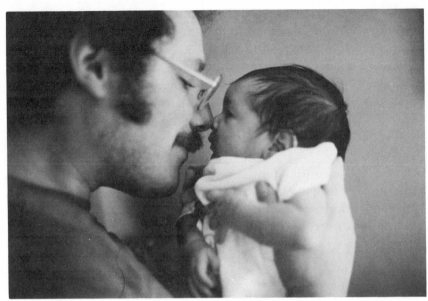

Courtesy of David Kliot, M.D.

5 · Development of Synchrony

With the recent impetus in infant research, we have become increasingly aware that the young infant is a great deal more capable of organized responses than has been assumed, and that he is not nearly the passive-receptive organism he has been described as for so long. We are beginning to learn that, by virtue of his earliest characteristics, he is an active contributor to the beginning mother-infant interaction.

Anneliese F. Korner, article in
The Effect of the Infant on Its Caregiver

In earlier chapters we observed that newborn babies already possess the sensory equipment to absorb inputs from their surroundings, and the rudiments of cortical function with which to deal with these inputs. That newborns are also capable of a considerable degree of behavioral organization is evident from the delicate interplay of activities involved in such ordinary acts as suckling (that is, rooting, grasping the nipple area, sucking, swallowing, breathing).

This kind of *intra*personal coordination, or "synchrony," is already apparent in many of the behaviors seen *in utero,* for example, the response of the fetus to touch. After birth, however, the infant has the additional task of adjusting her responses to suit those of her caregivers and the changing conditions of life outside the uterus. The development of *inter*personal synchrony is a necessary prelude to social interaction, as psychologist Rudolph Shaffer clearly points out: "If babies had no inborn preadaptation for interacting with others, social development could not take place as quickly as it does. At birth an infant is essentially an asocial being, in the sense that he still has no concept of people and responds only to crude features that may be inherent in other members of the species but are not exclusive to them. Yet just a few months later he not only has a concept of people, but he has begun the task of mastering the many social skills he will need as a member of his particular cultural group."[1]

Babies are innately equipped to assume a social role because without it, say the researchers, they would fail to develop normally and, in many instances, die. Deprived of contact with their mothers, infant monkeys first go into a panic state, then appear to grieve, exhibit aberrant behaviors, and finally lapse into a stupor. In the absence of early handling, caressing, and similar loving exchanges with other human beings, institutionalized babies at the turn of the century routinely died of marasmus, or "wasting" disease.

That under normal circumstances a human connection does develop is proof of the effectiveness of biological programming for newborn survival. Partly, this can be explained by simple physical compatibility within the mother-infant pair—the structural conformity of the baby's mouth to his mother's nipple is a good example. But there are more subtle forces at work, as well.

One is the pull of the newborn's appearance, that amalgam of appealing characteristics identified by ethologist Konrad Lorenz as "babyness." The young of all mammalian species requiring protection from elder members of the species in order to survive, Lorenz pointed out, share certain physical characteristics which seem to call forth caregiving responses.

Among these, Lorenz noted, are a head that is large in proportion to the baby's body, a protruding forehead, large eyes, and round, chubby cheeks. Other investigators have since commented on the tendency among advertisers of baby products to exaggerate these very features in drawings or photographs designed to call attention to their products. Psychologist Louise J. Kaplan adds: "The mottled skin of the newborn, his hairless body, unfocused eyes and uncoordinated body movements give him a helpless and vulnerable look. His vulnerable appearance makes a mother want to hold him and care for him." [2]

But the newborn's appearance is only half of the story. How the baby molds her face and body into expressive movements that delight—and form an actual communication network with—her parents is equally important. Although the age at which such infant behaviors as smiling, eye brightening, and babbling become truly socially motivated is matter for conjecture, they are seen by the parents as conveying friendliness right from the start. As child psychoanalyst and author Selma Fraiberg describes it: "During the first six months, the baby has the rudiments of a love language available to him. There is the language of the embrace, the language of the eyes, the language of the smile, vocal communications of pleasure and distress. It is the essential vocabulary of love before we can speak of love. Eighteen years later, when this baby is full grown and 'falls in love' for the first time, he will woo his partner through the language of the eyes, the language of the smile, through the utterance of endearments, and the joy of the embrace." [3]

Charles Darwin was the first to point out that newborns are innately equipped to communicate pleasure, anger, fear, joy, and disgust via their facial expressions, and that each of these cues is perceived by other members of the species as conveying a particular message. What the baby does with her anatomical endowment—whether she appears intelligent or dull, how often she looks pleased and how often she frowns—will form the basis of her parents' responses and affect their caretaking. The kind of stimulation they provide will, in turn, heavily determine the course of the ensuing relationship.

THE SMILING RESPONSE

"Smiling," Louise J. Kaplan notes, "is a universal human gesture . . . an indication of the bond between one human being and another."[4] For a new mother, her baby's smiles provide the clearest indication of his contentment and her success in her new role. Many observers have commented on the long-range effect of infant smiling behavior on parental attachment. It stands to reason that the parent who *enjoys* picking up an infant because of her smiles and coos will also respond more willingly to that baby's distress signals.

Years ago, it was thought that the motor pattern of smiling was a learned response to parental stimulus, particularly during the feeding situation. However, it is now believed that newborn smiling is instinctual*—a valuable asset from an evolutionary standpoint in calling forth protective responses from caregivers. The thrilled reactions expressed by the parents of those gentle birth babies who do display smiles during the first hour of life would certainly bear this out.

There is currently some controversy over the age at which infant smiling indicates awareness of surroundings. Psychiatrist Peter Wolff notes that fleeting "reflex" smiles are observable in babies from birth onward, generally during periods of irregular (REM) sleep or drowsiness. However, until about the fourth week of life, when the baby begins to smile selectively in recognition of her mother's voice, it has generally been assumed that these take place in a vacuum, that is, are unrelated to emotion. In fact, although Wolff acknowledges that brief smiles may be elicited by gentle stroking, subdued light, or soft sounds, particularly those of a high-pitched human voice, the accepted scientific view has

---

* Convincing evidence that smiling is an instinctual behavior has been gathered from recent studies of blind children during the first year of life. In the early months, even those infants who are totally blind and have never seen a smiling face will smile brightly upon hearing their mothers' voices and attempt to focus their eyes in the direction from which the sound emanates. However, the facial responsiveness of blind children gradually fades, beginning around the fourth to sixth month of life. It is assumed that some feedback from the caregivers is necessary if the full strength of the smiling response is to be preserved. Blind children do, of course, find other means of expressing their pleasure and affection, but there is no question that the warmth of eye-to-eye contact is sorely missed by sighted parents.

been that, in the words of investigator John Bowlby, "during the first three weeks the [smiling] response is so incomplete that it leaves the spectator wholly unmoved: in other words, it has no functional consequence."[5]

Were the spectators who remained "wholly unmoved" the baby's mother and father? I tend to doubt it. At any rate, there is some likelihood that, once again, the scientists have underestimated newborn capabilities for eliciting a response. Let's not forget that until recently it was assumed even by child-care experts that *all* infant smiles were really only grimaces caused by gas! As Lee Salk notes humorously: "I think the notion that gas makes a baby smile developed a long time ago when some baby smiled and coincidentally passed gas at the very same moment. Some professional who was observing immediately concluded that the gas caused a smile. The observation was then transmitted as gospel from person to person until it was so generally accepted that no one questioned it. Many ridiculous and unfounded bits of information have been accumulated and passed on in this way."[6]

Initially, of course, smiling, crying, and other innate behaviors are not goal-directed; that is, they are performed spontaneously with no expectation that a response will be forthcoming. However, every day that passes brings new evidence that under the right circumstances parental response is immediate.

In the very first hour of life, provided mother and baby are reasonably alert and external stimuli not overpowering, a chain of infant-parent-infant reactions is set up that lays the groundwork for all future communication.

ENTRAINMENT

A chain is composed of individual links with at least some air space in between. Human communication would be impossible if all the participants spoke at once. There must be a fine-tuned rhythm regulating each individual's timing, and pauses during which the changeover from one actor to another can take place. How does a newborn baby learn to take part in such a complex interplay? Investigators have shown that just as the baby's mouth is structurally adapted to grasping her mother's nipple, her natural rhythms are ready at birth to be attuned to those of her caregivers.

The process by which inborn rhythms become adapted to conditions in the environment is known as "entrainment." (Common examples include the baby's adoption of a twenty-four-hour sleep-wake cycle and the adaptation of hunger rhythms to a structured feeding schedule.) That such apparently difficult adjustments are in fact made very rapidly may appear surprising, until one considers that even *in utero* many of the fetus's behaviors are synchronized with those of her mother. It is believed that the basic on-off rhythm pattern which makes possible the enmeshing of infant and maternal behaviors is common to all human beings; indeed, interpersonal dialogue of any kind hardly seems conceivable without such a shared pattern.

Babies move their heads, eyes, and torsos in synchrony with adult speech from birth onward. Detailed film analyses of three-month-olds and their mothers by psychiatrist Daniel Stern show a remarkable dialogue of split-second cues and responses, in which the mother allows the baby to take the lead, then follows with a word or gesture designed to produce further interaction.

Although she is unaware of her role much of the time, it is the mother's ability to interpret her infant's signals and respond appropriately that provides the guarantee that this "dance" will proceed smoothly. When mothers are deprived of the opportunity to become sufficiently acquainted with their babies, missteps can occur, as we shall see in later chapters. But first, let's examine some of the features that contribute to the healthy establishment of interpersonal synchrony.

Responsiveness to human speech. Newborns react to the sounds produced by human speech far more readily than to other frequencies or pure tones. One- to two-day-old babies in one test moved synchronously with adult speakers when addressed in both English and Chinese, but not when exposed to either tapping noises or disconnected vowel sounds. Responsiveness to speech patterns not only prepares the infant for acquisition of language later in development, it also provides the caregiver with welcome reinforcement for further verbal interaction.

Gaze.

This first look is unforgettable. Immense, deep, grave, intense, these eyes say: "Where am I? What has happened to me?" We feel in this baby such utter concentration, such astonishment, such depth of curiosity, that we are overcome. We discover that beyond any doubt, a *person* is there.[7]

It was not so long ago that pediatric textbooks made light of the claims of excited new mothers that their babies could see them. Today we know that newborn infants not only can see without prior learning experience, but can also follow and fixate upon a moving object, as long as the object is within their visual field. The inhospitality of overlit hospital environments to early visual exploration, and the fact that the visual field of a very tiny infant is quite limited when compared to that of an adult (objects outside a range of roughly eight to twelve inches become increasingly blurred), were responsible for the mistaken assumption that newborn babies could not see at all.

How important this ability of the newborn's actually is may be guessed from the fact that eight inches is almost precisely the distance between the infant's eyes and those of her mother when the two are in normal breast- or bottle-feeding position. The relation of early eye-to-eye contact and the sense of recognition this produces to the deepening of parental attachment has been pointed out by a number of investigators.

T. Berry Brazelton notes that when the pediatrician attaches importance to the infant's visual capacity and the ability of the mother and father to respond in kind, he affirms them as observant, caring parents and increases their self-confidence. "It also seems to me," Brazelton writes, "that we have 'allowed' them to think of their new baby as a person in his own right. And that may be quite critical to their perception of him as a vital, exciting individual."[8]

What babies choose to look at is equally revealing. Repeated experiments have demonstrated that infants, when given a choice between a variety of forms and a line drawing of a human face, will inevitably choose to fixate on the face, particularly when this is presented so that the eyes (or dots representing them) are visible. Newborns also exhibit a preference for correctly drawn faces over faces which have been scrambled, and are able to imitate the exaggerated facial expressions of adults with remarkable accuracy —to the great amusement of onlookers.

If, as researchers now believe, babies are born with an innate preference for the human face over other forms, this provides yet another suggestion that our genetic makeup predisposes us to interact as social animals with others of our species. "Eye-to-eye contact," says Louise J. Kaplan, "is an important component of human communication. What we do with our eyes becomes a measure of how friendly or close we feel toward another human being—turning the eyes away, averting the gaze, looking directly in the eyes, or closing the eyes altogether in order to maintain a state of intense intimacy."[9]

Crying. We have already discussed the power of the newborn smiling response to initiate caretaking behaviors from nearby adults. The same holds true of the other extreme. Loud crying is a phenomenally effective means of making sure that the baby's wants are attended to, that she is fed, kept warm and dry, or simply loved and cuddled. Although the newborn has a range of cries which she selectively uses when hungry, angry, frustrated, or in pain, only the last of the group—the pain cry—elicits a predictable adult response. Whether the mother is from New York, London, or the Kalahari Desert in Africa, a baby's pain cry is certain to be heeded. And in picking up and soothing the infant, the caretaker offers yet another opportunity for alert observation and social exchange.

Quiet, alert state. In 1959, Peter Wolff defined six separate states of consciousness in the newborn: quiet sleep, active sleep, drowsiness, quiet alertness, active alertness, and crying. Of these six, the fourth, or quiet, alert state, has held the most fascination for subsequent observers.

In this state the infant's eyes are wide open. Wild, uncoordinated body movements cease; the baby calmly gazes about and responds to her parents' looks and gestures with interest.

In their ground-breaking study of maternal-infant bonding, pediatricians Marshall H. Klaus and John H. Kennell suggest that the difficulty of getting newborns to *maintain* this state for any length of time was a major factor in its late detection. However, the same investigators add that such difficulty does not appear to affect responsiveness at one "sensitive" period: that is, during the first forty-five to sixty minutes after birth. At that time, babies delivered by unmedicated childbirth remain awake and alert, will turn their heads to the spoken word, and may follow their mothers visually over an arc of 180 degrees or more. After about an hour of such responsiveness, the baby goes into a deep sleep for three or four hours, and may remain drowsy for some days afterward.

Their conclusion: that the period immediately after birth provides a unique opportunity for exchange of gaze and the initiation of dialogue between parent and child.

NOTES

1. Rudolph Schaffer, *Mothering* (Cambridge, Mass.: Harvard University Press, 1977), pp. 62–63.
2. Louise J. Kaplan, *Oneness and Separateness: From Infant to Individual* (New York: Simon & Schuster, 1978), p. 73.
3. Selma Fraiberg, *Every Child's Birthright: In Defense of Mothering* (New York: Basic Books, 1977), p. 29.
4. Kaplan, *Oneness and Separateness,* p. 74.
5. John Bowlby, *Attachment,* Vol. 1 (New York: Basic Books, 1969), p. 281.
6. Lee Salk, *Preparing for Parenthood* (New York, David McKay, 1974), p. 113.
7. Leboyer, *Birth Without Violence,* p. 78.
8. T. Berry Brazelton, "The Miracle of Birth: How Babies See Their World," *Redbook,* March 1978, p. 188.
9. Kaplan, *Oneness and Separateness,* p. 78.

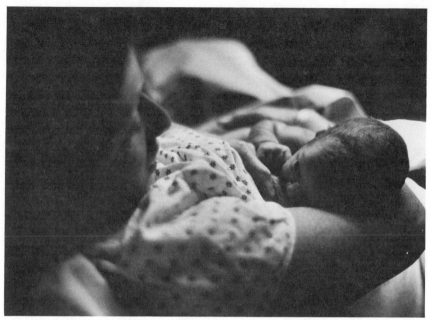

Courtesy of David Kliot, M.D.

6 · The Roots of Attachment

From numerous clinical experiences we believe that an essential principle of attachment is that parents must receive some response or signal, such as body or eye movements from their infant, to form a close bond. . . . We have abbreviated this principle to: "You cannot fall in love with a dishrag."

Marshall H. Klaus and
John H. Kennell,
Maternal-Infant Bonding

After studying hundreds of babies and their parents, Klaus and Kennell decided that there appears to exist a sensitive period in the first hour or so of life, during which close contact between

THE GENTLE BIRTH BOOK

mother, father, and newborn may help to ensure that later development is optimal.

This is not to say, the researchers emphasize, that extended contact with the baby in the days and months following birth will have no effect on attachment, or even that the absence of immediate contact will be clearly detrimental. Love between parents and children is not instinctual; it does not happen overnight. (Klaus and Kennell call this misinterpretation of their work the "epoxy" theory.)

There is, instead, a gradual deepening of attachment based on communication and growth of mutual respect. The stirrings of empathy felt by many women in early pregnancy increase with fetal movement and are enriched by events that take place during and after delivery, when the baby is brought home from the hospital, and for many years afterward. As for the infant, she loves because she is loved by her parents—whether natural or adoptive. There is no magic moment for bonding to take place.

Nevertheless, since the chief benefit of gentle childbirth lies in providing an atmosphere in which parents and newborn babies can get acquainted without interruption, it is worthwhile to examine the evidence for a sensitive period, and also see what may happen when parents are *denied* the opportunity to begin parenting at the biologically appropriate time.

A SENSITIVE PERIOD

In the previous section we saw how the innate ability of the newborn to adapt to his caregivers' patterns had enormous evolutionary value in protecting the weak infant from predators and ensuring that his basic needs for food, warmth, and contact comfort were met. Does the baby's particular readiness for dialogue during the first hour of life serve a similar purpose? In addition to evidence derived from studies of attachment behavior in animals, researchers have uncovered specific biological mechanisms which, during the period immediately following birth, both encourage maternal responsiveness and reduce the danger of infection in the human newborn.

Biological mechanisms. It is believed that certain hormonal changes in the final stages of labor create a climate of heightened awareness in which the mother is particularly receptive to her baby's signals, around the time of birth.

Suckling the infant after birth stimulates maternal secretion of the pituitary hormones prolactin and oxytocin, the former promoting lactation, the latter, in addition to initiating the milk "letdown" reflex, encouraging uterine contraction and completion of the third stage of labor—detachment of the placenta. Oxytocin also acts to reduce postpartum bleeding and danger of maternal hemorrhage.

The benefits conferred on the baby by the colostrum secreted by his mother's breasts, particularly with regard to immunity against various strains of pathogenic organisms, are well-known. Less well-known is the possibility that early physical contact may *in itself* afford substantial protection against infection. Klaus and Kennell suggest that if mother and baby are allowed to remain together in the first minutes of life, the mother will transmit to the newborn her own mixture of strains of respiratory organisms, such as Staphylococcus, which then grow and populate the infant's respiratory and gastrointestinal tracts.

"Just as a lawn planted with grass will resist the introduction of weeds after the grass has had a good start," say the investigators, "these organisms may prevent the baby from acquiring the hospital strains of staphylococci."[1]

Imprinting in animals. In the early part of this century, scientists were unanimous in believing that babies became attached to their caretakers as a response to being fed by them. The need for human interchange was considered a "secondary" drive, subordinate to the basic needs for nourishment, shelter, sex, and so forth.

Then, in 1935, Konrad Lorenz published some findings about the behavior of young ducklings and goslings which were to shatter this theory and lead other investigators to reach new conclusions about the nature of attachment in man. Lorenz reported that the baby birds tended to fixate upon the first moving object they saw after being hatched—whether mother bird, a rubber balloon, or Lorenz himself—and follow that object from that moment on, even without benefit of food or other encouragement. Once such an attachment had been formed, it was irreversible; the "imprinting" that occurred in the first moments of a young bird's life would affect all of its subsequent behavior patterns, determine its choice of a mate, and so forth.

While Lorenz was firm in stating that imprinting had no counterpart among mammalian species, other investigators have dis-
puted this conclusion. Gradually, the concept of imprinting was
broadened to include any clearly defined preference for a "love
object" that develops rather quickly in a young animal and, once
fixed, remains comparatively stable.

The existence of a maternal responsive period in mammals was
confirmed by a number of studies in the 1950s and 1960s. Separation of mother goats, sheep, and cattle from their young after
parturition almost inevitably resulted in rejection of the offspring
later on. The role of physical contact between mother and newborn was found to be crucial. Monkeys allowed to see, but not
touch, their young gradually lost all interest in them; baby lambs
who were not licked by their mothers shortly after birth failed to
thrive.

Of course, human beings are not geese, monkeys, or sheep.
Just how relevant, the investigators wondered, would the animal
studies of imprinting behavior prove to be to the far more complex relationship between human mothers and their infants?

Human attachments: first contacts. Did a critical period for maternal-infant bonding analogous to that in birds and lower mammals
(although not nearly so irrevocable) also exist in man? The
thought occurred to Klaus and Kennell during their investigations of disorders in parenting.

The researchers noticed that the parents of certain children
who began life with some minor irregularity (say, jaundice), which
was then corrected and did not recur, *continued* to regard those
children with concern and treat them with special care and
attention as they grew to adulthood. The pattern persisted regardless of the child's current state of good health and the considerable damage that such overprotection might do to his
emerging self-concept. First impressions, it appeared, counted
to an extraordinary degree in producing these "vulnerable"
children.

(To cite a somewhat different and more serious example: the
infant who began life as a small premature and who, although
now a strapping five-year-old, might still be regarded as a "weak-
ling" by his parents and siblings, and taunted or physically abused
on that account.)

It had been observed for some time by those involved in caring for high-risk infants that a disproportionate number of newborns whose lives had been spared by medical miracles would later be readmitted to the hospital as battered babies and children. Noting the apparent correlation of prematurity with both failure-to-thrive* in the early months and outright child abuse later on, Klaus and Kennell examined their own practices, and found that many of the mothers whose babies had been hustled off to incubators immediately after birth would be looking out of the window or leafing through a magazine during the child's one-month checkup . . . rather than standing at the pediatrician's elbow to watch and comfort. In the years that followed, many of these same children would turn up at the emergency room, time and time again, with "accidental" burns and bruises.

The Ohio investigators decided to explore the effects on maternal-infant interaction when postpartum contact was actively encouraged—rather than being discouraged or denied outright as had become the case in many maternity units, for normal full-term as well as premature births.

In their first study of early extended contact, two groups of fourteen primiparous (first-time) mothers and their full-term infants were compared. The first group of mothers were given their nude babies in bed for one hour within two hours after birth† and for five additional hours on each of three successive days. The second, control group of mothers received "routine" care consisting of a glimpse of the baby at birth, a second brief visit at six to eight hours of life, then visits of twenty to thirty minutes for feedings every four hours.

One month later, each mother's responses to her infant were assessed by means of a standardized interview, observation of that mother's behavior during the infant's physical examination, and a filmed study of a typical bottle-feeding situation. The two groups of mothers were then reassessed in a shorter observation period after one year, and additional testing was done at two and five years.

---

* A disorder in which the newborn fails to develop normally or gain weight (without apparent organic cause) at home, yet recovers rapidly when given only standard hospital care.
† It is interesting to speculate that differences seen in the two groups might have been even *greater* had the mothers been allowed to remain with their babies from birth onward, as was the practice in subsequent studies and is the norm in gentle births.

Considering that a total of only sixteen hours of extra contact was involved in all, the results were astonishing. Extended contact mothers were much more reluctant to leave their infants with other caretakers and generally stood and watched during the physical examination. When the babies cried, the extended contact mothers were the first to soothe and comfort. Although both groups spent an equivalent amount of time looking at their babies in the feeding situation, mothers in the extended contact group met their infants' eyes more fully (*en face*), caressed them more frequently, and fed them more expertly than did control mothers.

Other studies in developing countries have shown fewer episodes of infection and more rapid weight gain in babies allowed early contact with their mothers. In one experiment, six mothers who were given their babies to suckle shortly after birth were compared with six mothers who had begun nursing approximately sixteen hours later. All mothers had planned to breast-feed and none encountered physical problems; yet two months later only one mother among those in the "late" group was still breast feeding, in contrast to all six of the mothers in the "early" group!

Another important study by Peter de Chateau in Umea, Sweden, showed that *even a single extra hour* of naked skin-to-skin and suckling contact immediately after birth between infants and primiparous mothers resulted in notable behavioral changes at thirty-six hours after birth and again at three months. Mothers allowed the additional contact during the first postpartum hour showed more holding, encompassing, direct gazing, and (at three months) more kissing of their infants than mothers given routine hospital care. For their part, infants responded to the extra early contact by smiling more and crying less frequently at the three-month observation. (See chart.)

De Chateau concludes: "The relatively short period of extra contact during the first hour following delivery can perhaps not completely explain the differences in maternal and infant behavior later on. Mothers and infants during this early contact might, however, have had an opportunity to exchange signals, which may be of importance for the establishment of mother-infant synchrony. Consequently the development of the mother-infant relationship may proceed more smoothly."[2]

Maternal (upper) and infant (lower) behavior 3 months after delivery during a home visit.

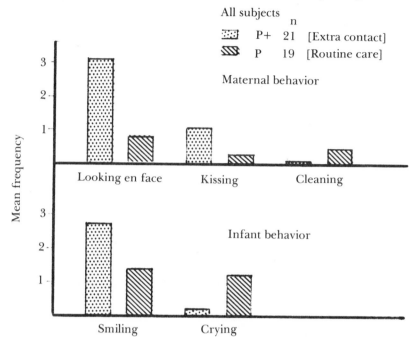

SOURCE: *Birth and the Family Journal* 3:4 (1976). Used by permission.

GROWTH OF EMPATHY

One doesn't have to look too far to find clinical support for the sensitive period hypothesis. In cases where hospitals have accidentally given one mother the child of another to care for, then discovered and attempted to right the mistake, the mother's response has frequently been reluctance to part with the baby she has nursed or even held briefly after birth. Even when given their own infants to nurture, these women continued to think of the first baby with tenderness and remorse.

Certainly, the consistency with which the parents of gentle birth babies refer to these infants' initial responsiveness (with remarks like: "He looked right at us and seemed to be questioning who we were. But then his face relaxed. . . . I think he approved.") testifies to the contribution such intimate early contact can make to the developing relationship.

But again, human babies are not goslings. It takes far more than a single positive meeting to produce a love relationship, as Selma Fraiberg points out: "The bond which is ensured in a moment of time between a baby animal and its mother is, in the case of the human baby, the product of a complex sequential development, a process that evolves during the first eighteen months of life. The instinctual patterns are elicited through the human environment, but they do not take the form of instinctual release phenomena in terms of a code and its unlocking. What we see in the evolution of the human bond is a language between partners . . . in which messages from the infant are interpreted by his mother and messages from the mother are taken as signals by the baby. This early dialogue of 'need' and 'an answer to need' becomes a highly differentiated signal system in the early months of life; it is, properly speaking, the matrix of human language and of the human bond itself."[3]

A new mother's attitude toward her infant is affected by her own cultural conditioning and childhood memories, past and present relationship with her parents, relationship with her husband, whether the pregnancy was planned or unplanned, events in the prenatal course, outcome of any previous pregnancies, her age, general health, financial status, and a hundred other variables. Although paternal behavior has been less well studied, it appears that similar factors tend to influence the behavior of both parents—or, for that matter, any primary caretaker.

The great advantage of early interaction is that it gives the caretakers a chance to become attuned to their baby's individuality, with the result that signals are interpreted correctly from the start and fewer misunderstandings occur. Anneliese Korner notes that family life proceeds at a much smoother pace if the mother accepts her baby's basic temperament and allows her responses to be governed by whether he is passive or excitable, cuddly or resistant to cuddling.

This is particularly important in the case of primiparous mothers, who, in our fragmented society, come into the relationship with hardly any experience in dealing with tiny infants and none of the self-assurance that such experience ordinarily brings.

The second time around. Child-care experts all agree: bringing up baby is easier the second time around. An expectant mother leafing through Dr. Benjamin Spock's classic *Baby and Child Care* will come across this passage: "A mother is apt to say, 'The second baby is so easy. He doesn't cry. He is rarely a serious problem. He plays contentedly by himself, and yet he is so friendly if you go near him.' "[4]

Why should this be so? The major factor blamed by Spock and other authorities for the difficulty with first children is that inexperienced parents tend to take their job too seriously. They just try too hard. He explains: "You know what I mean if you have ever seen a tense person trying to ride a horse for the first time. He sits stiff as a china doll, doesn't know how to accommodate to the horse's movements, and is apt to be unnecessarily bossy. It's hard work for the horse and the rider. The experienced rider knows how to relax, how to give in and conform to some of the horse's motions without losing his seat, how to direct the horse gently. Bringing up a child isn't much like riding a horse, but the same spirit works in both jobs."[5]

What do parents learn in bringing up their first child? Not just how to change a diaper or bandage a skinned knee, but a sense of basic competence, a knack for reading between the lines, and some understanding of what the world looks like from a child's point of view.

Interestingly, that sense of being utterly overwhelmed by the baby's incessant demands for food and attention, the ever-present pile of laundry, and the need to continue caring for other members of the household (including oneself) which is so common among Western mothers has no counterpart in less-developed nations. During the endless, tragic conflict in Southeast Asia, the sight of teenage girls effectively assuming responsibility for the care of entire extended families became sadly commonplace to American soldiers and news personnel. And in their studies of young Guatemalan women, Klaus and Kennell noted the ease with which older children in the rural Indian villages cared for infant brothers and sisters, and the opportunity this offered a girl "to make fine adjustments in her mothering style and gain a wealth of confidence"[6] before actually becoming a mother herself.

In a nuclear family structure, by contrast, the unfamiliarity of first-time parents with the basics of infant care—and their subsequent heavy reliance on how-to books—can almost be taken for granted.* It appears, however, that there may be ways of counteracting this unique form of cultural deprivation. Childbirth education and parenting programs have proved extremely effective means of educating young expectant couples about birth and providing welcome group support during the baby's formative years. And, as the various studies of early extended contact illustrate, the ability to exchange signals in the postpartum period offers new parents a marvelous opportunity to get the relationship off to a good start. Comments Grover: "There is an air of confidence in facing the challenges of early parenting [with gentle birth], almost as though the learning experiences of a prior pregnancy had been incorporated and the parents had 'been there' many times before."

WHEN ATTACHMENT FAILS:
Beyond the Limits of Adaptability

Mothers separated from their young soon lost all interest in those whom they were unable to nurse or cherish.

Pierre Budin, *The Nursling*, 1907

Until this entire country gets back into the family business, we are on a headlong course for disaster in terms of human relationships and family interaction.

L. Joseph Butterfield, M.D.
former chairman, Committee on Maternal and Child Care,
American Medical Association Council on Scientific Affairs, 1977

The second half of the twentieth century has provided the setting for two divergent trends in American obstetrical care. One has been the increasing systematization of hospital birth encouraged by the growth of large regional centers, generally located

---

* Playing with dolls—whether their skins are rigid or flexible, whether they "wet" or do not "wet"—can hardly be said to give little girls a sense of what caring for another, defenseless human being is like. And little boys in our culture are not afforded even this primitive opportunity at caretaking!

within an urban teaching hospital framework, designed to meet the needs of high-risk expectant mothers and their babies.

Although this was not the original intent, continuing regionalization of care has cut deeply into the obstetrical practices of family physicians and helped to empty the maternity units of many smaller and presumably less-well-equipped community hospitals (in much the same way, ironically, as the growth of the medical specialty of obstetrics stripped American midwives of their function around the turn of the century).

There is no denying that—costly as the sophisticated emergency services offered by the centers are for both the recipients and providers of care—they have already saved thousands of lives. Many small premature and other high-risk infants are healthy today, who only a few years ago would have been permanently damaged or lost due to respiratory distress or inadequate postpartum intensive care.

Despite these obvious advances, however, it has become increasingly clear as the 1970s draw to a close that all is not love and roses in American maternity hospitals.

What has happened?

Simply that alongside the elaborate tools designed to make certain that the babies born are healthy babies—and the emergence of a whole new subspecialty of neonatology to deal with the infant at risk—has come the disquieting realization that some of those very technologic breakthroughs tend to play havoc with parental-infant attachment.

It seems that the treatment of normal expectant women as "patients" requiring enforced bed rest, surgical preparation, elaborate monitoring equipment, separation from their older children (and on occasion even separation from their husbands) invites feelings of helplessness and inadequacy and reinforces fears of a possible bad outcome.

Similarly, excessive use of pain-deadening medication during labor and delivery, in addition to increasing the likelihood of respiratory difficulties in the fetus, creates a listlessness in both mother and baby that limits opportunities for bonding and discourages early suckling. Overbright operating-room lights and immediate application of silver nitrate drops further delay establishment of eye contact. Immediate removal of the infant to a nursery, followed by rigid visiting/feeding schedules and the of-

THE GENTLE BIRTH BOOK

fering of supplemental bottles by nursing staff combine to effectively thwart breast feeding and inhibit the normal exchange of
signals between baby and mother. The complete picture is one of
isolation of the newborn from his parents and the undermining
of any confidence the couple may have had in their parenting
abilities.

The correlation between the isolation of premature babies and
both failure-to-thrive syndrome and child abuse has already been
discussed. Less extreme, but equally unfortunate, have been the
damaging effects of the pathologic model ("you are sick until
proven well") as this has been applied to healthy pregnancies and
perfectly routine births.

Thus, the second trend in obstetrics, the search for alternatives
in childbearing, began as a reaction against the first . . . or, rather,
against the threat of emotional deprivation that many aspects of
institutionalized care pose to the families affected by them.

Baby blues . . . or worse. Having little to do in such a setting except
recuperate from the effects of anesthesia and dwell upon the
discomfort caused by her episiotomy stitches (in all likelihood
acquired as a direct result of her inability to push), the young
mother becomes increasingly downcast and apprehensive. Deprived of supportive relatives and, far more importantly, of a
baby to nurture, yet convinced* that she is ill-equipped to assume
his care, she begins to dread the day of discharge from the hospital. Already on the postpartum floor, the preconditions are set
for postnatal depression, that civilized malady known as the "baby
blues."

"Consider a mother suffering from postnatal depression," says
Rudolph Schaffer. "She sits apathetically with her baby on her
knee, staring vacantly around her and hardly noticing his behavior. He wriggles uncomfortably, but she takes no action to mold
her body to his; he whimpers but she fails to investigate the cause
of his distress. There is no feeling in anything she does, she is
drained of emotion and quite incapable of any involvement with
her offspring. The constant flow of his behavior means nothing
to her: his responses have no signal value, for she is too encapsu-
lated in her own feelings to be aware of the child's."[7]

---

* At this point, with considerable justification.

When the day of discharge finally arrives, both parents feel a sense of confusion and unreality that may, even under the best of circumstances, persist for weeks to come. "Who is this tiny, demanding stranger?" they wonder. "What relation does he have to us?"

Several investigators have noted that women who have been separated from their infants at birth often appear especially hesitant and clumsy when first attempting such simple tasks as feeding and diapering. When the separation is prolonged, the mother may occasionally forget that she even has a baby, and during the first month at home continue to think of the infant as "belonging" to the hospital personnel, rather than to herself.

Where a lengthy stay in the intensive care nursery has been unavoidable, mothers denied contact with their infants during this period are almost uniform in expressing a sense of guilt, as though the baby's prematurity, malformation, or other problem might be attributable to some careless act of their own during pregnancy. Concern about being able to protect the infant from harm may extend well into the homecoming period, with both parents admitting reluctance to bathe the baby (for fear that she might drown), dress her (she could break an arm), and so forth.

In truly pathologic cases, the mother of a small premature baby may become so numbed by fear that the child will not survive the hospital stay that she literally avoids all contact that might result in formation of an emotional tie. Ordinary "nesting" behaviors, such as painting the baby's bedroom, buying the layette, and the mailing of birth announcements are notably absent. If a long period of special care is required *and the hospital fails to actively encourage contact,* withdrawal of investment in the child may be great enough to permanently damage the relationship.

In one study, Klaus and Kennell found that when nesting behaviors were encouraged—by permitting mothers to live in with their premature infants and provide basic caretaking before discharge, allowing fathers unlimited visiting privileges, a comfortable chair and a cot to sleep on, and so forth—the parents' caretaking skills and confidence improved greatly. A number of other studies have revealed that simple cuddling, rocking, and stroking of the newborn during the nursery stay result in improved respiration and weight gain, and that increased eye contact with the parents correlates with higher IQ scores. The encouragement of mothers to begin supplying breast milk to their premature infants has been clearly shown to both reduce the number of infections and other complications in the newborn and encourage maternal-infant attachment.

That certain enlightened hospital administrators are beginning to think in terms of fostering the emotional health, as well as mere survival, of premature and other high-risk infants is certainly commendable. That in many other institutions research findings on attachment continue to be ignored, with the result that even normal mothers and healthy full-term babies are often needlessly subjected to isolationary intensive care procedures, is inexcusable:

Throughout most of human history, anatomic, physiologic, and behavioral adaptations within the mother-infant relationship have been capable of providing the nutrition, protection, and social stimulation necessary for the infant's survival and development. Perinatal medical care was introduced in this century with the purpose of further decreasing mortality and morbidity by preventing infection and managing physical problems. There is now a growing body of evidence that these advances inadvertently alter the initiation of the mother-infant relationship and that some mother-infant pairs may be strained beyond limits of their adaptability.[8]

Leboyer-inspired nonviolence is clearly one of several related steps away from mechanization and toward a more humanistic approach to childbearing. In the following chapter, we will explore each of the components of gentle birth in greater detail and show how, without the slightest sacrifice of safety, together they contribute to arrest the damage done by the earlier trend.

NOTES

1. Marshall H. Klaus and John H. Kennell, *Maternal-Infant Bonding* (St. Louis: C. V. Mosby, 1976), p. 76.
2. Peter de Chateau, "The Influence of Early Contact on Maternal and Infant Behaviour in Primiparae," *Birth and the Family Journal* 3 (1976): 154–55.
3. Selma Fraiberg, *Every Child's Birthright: In Defense of Mothering* (New York: Basic Books, 1977), p. 57.
4. Benjamin Spock, *Baby and Child Care*, rev. ed. (New York: Pocket Books, 1968), p. 312.

5. Ibid., p. 313.
6. Klaus and Kennell, *Maternal-Infant Bonding,* p. 40.
7. Rudolph Schaffer, *Mothering* (Cambridge, Mass.: Harvard University Press, 1977), p. 81.
8. Betsy Lozoff, Gary M. Brittenham, Mary Anne Trause, John H. Kennell, and Marshall H. Klaus, "The Mother-Newborn Relationship: Limits of Adaptability," *Journal of Pediatrics,* July 1977, p. 1.

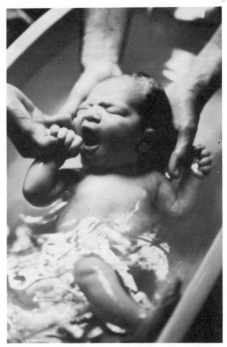

Courtesy of David Kliot, M.D.

7 · How Nonviolence Works

. . . by attending to the new parents' needs and wishes and by not snowing the baby so he can't be responsive, we allow for a very different kind of bonding to be available.

T. Berry Brazelton, M.D.

What makes a gentle birth? Nine elements spring to mind:

- A nurturing, family-centered setting for birth, with avoidance of unnecessary medical intervention
- Preparation for childbirth and minimal use of sense-deadening medication

- A subdued environment—darkened and quieted to the extent that this is feasible
- Delayed clamping of the umbilical cord until pulsations have ceased
- Placement of the newborn in a postural drainage position in direct skin-to-skin contact with his mother
- Gentle massage of the baby by both parents
- A water bath in which the father's role predominates
- Laying the baby at his mother's breast to nurse
- Extended contact, with opportunities for parental-infant visual, auditory, and tactile exchanges, during the recovery period and throughout the hospital stay

Let's take a moment to reexamine each in turn.

WATCHING A FAMILY GROW

We tell prospective parents that *they* are having this baby. The obstetrical staff is merely their insurance policy.

David Kliot, M.D.

The human touch. Nonviolent birth is definitely incompatible with the kind of assembly-line arrangement in which one nurse is responsible for looking after four or five women in labor and an obstetrician arrives at the last minute—if he arrives in time at all —to "catch" the baby and stitch up the mother.

Not only is this kind of setting hardly conducive to promoting a caring atmosphere, it is also medically unsound. Even where electronic fetal monitoring is in use, the equipment is only as good as the personnel available to interpret it. And the fact of the matter is that a simple stethoscope in the hands of a qualified obstetrician, midwife, or obstetrical nurse responsible for the care of *that patient alone* is an equally effective monitoring device in normal pregnancies.

When such factors as Pitocin induction, potential or actual fetal distress, and/or the likelihood of cesarean section provide clear medical indications for electronic surveillance, the purpose of the machinery and the necessity for restricting the laboring woman's freedom of movement should be explained to the couple in advance. (Most couples require some reassurance that the magnified sound of the baby's heartbeat is not in itself cause for alarm.) Those who have taken Lamaze training can be shown how to use the monitors to tell when a contraction is building up and when the peak has passed. Since universal electronic monitoring appears to be the wave of the future—already in some large teaching institutions, over 90 percent of patients are automatically "wired up," no matter how uneventful the pregnancy—a way must be found to make the laboring woman feel more like a mother and less like a computer terminal.

The problem with electronic fetal monitoring, insist the critics, extends beyond the intimidating appearance of the equipment and the limitations placed on mobility. Machines tend to displace human contact, and human contact is vital to childbearing. Physical support for the woman in labor—in the form of touching, stroking, back rubs, abdominal pressure, verbal encouragement, even chanting—has a tradition lasting as long as human history.*

It is believed by many sensitive observers that, behind their efficiency and stainless-steel glitter, medical interventions such as the monitors and routine IV have stripped modern birth of its dignity and ritual, leaving only the discomfort and fear. What began thousands of years ago as a rite of initiation into the human community has become instead a rather ordinary surgical procedure, in which the baby's emotional needs are ignored and his parents play only a very minor supporting role.

One indication of the "uneventfulness" of modern birth is the way in which obstetrics is regarded by most obstetricians. The consensus seems to be that delivering babies—always with the notable exception of those cases labeled "high-risk"—offers no challenge at all. Obstetrician-gynecologists frequently regard the former half of their specialty as work for novices, and prefer to concentrate on the latter as soon as their practices can afford it.

We are happy to say that in certain respects this response is justified. Most births are uncomplicated; with the perinatal mortality rate down around 1 percent, obstetrics today offers few opportunities for operating-room heroics.

---

* It is interesting to consider that in being able to provide this kind of intimate support throughout the course of labor and delivery, the midwife has a clear advantage over the technologically oriented obstetrician. In fact, safety records for certified nurse-midwives in this country have been outstanding.

However, we respectfully suggest that there are challenges of an entirely different sort to be met, as this comment by a grateful mother of two illustrates: "I had lost a child between my four-year-old and this baby, and let me tell you: I was scared. Having my doctor in the birthing room with me, checking the fetal heartbeat every few minutes and telling me, 'You're fine. Your baby's fine,' really made a tremendous difference. I calmed down. I felt I was prepared, I was in control."

Critics of nonviolent birth complain that it tends to be time-consuming. After all, the doctor has to prepare the patient beforehand, or at least see to it that she receives outside instruction in the form of childbirth education and demonstrations of baby massage. And then there is all that waiting around while the baby gradually opens his eyes, learns to move about, and discovers the wonder of his body.

Furthermore, it is likely that the physician or midwife who specializes in this approach will also spend additional time in the labor room, helping the couple over the difficult passages with a word here, a touch there, explaining the rationale for each procedure and ready to discuss the pros and cons of anesthesia as the need arises.

More time-consuming? A little, no doubt, for what director would begrudge his actors a few extra moments of rehearsal on opening night? And then, like any good director, he steps back into the dimly lit area behind the scenes, to wait and watch. Because, after all, it's their show. . . .

"Observe a gentle delivery in action, and what do you see?" John Grover asks. "You see a family at work—growing!"

Home or hospital? Outraged by the insensitive treatment accorded healthy mothers and newborns in hospitals, an increasing number of expectant parents have, during the past ten years, opted to give birth at home. Reasons offered are numerous, ranging from the comfort of the woman's own bed and the opportunity for older children and grandparents to be present, to the substantial difference in cost. Raven Lang, a midwife who has extensively studied home birth, notes the control displayed by the laboring woman and how the joyous, holiday atmosphere of the baby's arrival affects all who witness it. The observers also become remarkably attached to the infant, a phenomenon which Klaus and Kennell believe had considerable survival value in ensuring a substitute caretaker, back in the days when maternal mortality was higher.

Clearly, the chances for early bonding are increased by the greater opportunities available for prolonged gaze, verbal and tactile exchanges, and immediate introduction of the baby to the breast. What, then, is wrong with home birth?

First let's take the simplest case: an uncomplicated pregnancy and childbirth. The question that immediately arises is, "Who will attend the delivery?" Finding a qualified obstetrician or family physician willing to tackle a home birth is nearly impossible. Certified nurse-midwives are in short supply; most are currently affiliated with hospital maternity units or birthing centers. As for the growing contingent of lay midwives, their background and experience may consist of anything from extensive European training to a few self-help courses at the local women's center.

Of course, convincing evidence is offered by both sides. In one large study, researchers from Stanford University and the University of California followed 287 women who gave birth at home with the aid of lay midwives from the Santa Cruz Birth Center. Results were very satisfactory: the rate of postpartum infection was comparable to that associated with hospital births and the rate of complications was actually lower than in the population at large. However, the study population consisted exclusively of middle-class women, all of whom were well-fed, were educated for childbirth, received excellent prenatal care, and gave birth attended by two midwives! Furthermore, the conditions cited by the research team as contributing to the low perinatal mortality and morbidity—childbirth preparation, avoidance of medication, choice of semisitting, kneeling, or side-lying positions for birth rather than the old-fashioned supine delivery position, and the general absence of obstetrical interference—are not limited to home births but may be achieved in any family-centered maternity setting, without the sacrifice of safety should complications arise.

The danger of unexpected complications, of a sudden crisis requiring resuscitation of the infant or blood transfusion of the mother, constitutes the greatest argument against home birth. While it is true that a small percentage of the childbearing population account for the majority of losses, and also that the more serious complications such as diabetes or pregnancy-induced hypertension (toxemia) are generally identifiable in advance, there is always that small chance that, in the last minute, something may go wrong. With emergency services close by, the parents know that everything possible is being done to help. But without hospital backup (and in the absence of such well-organized mobile ambulance units as exist in certain European countries), tragedies can and do happen.

In January of 1978, the American College of Obstetricians and Gynecologists released a compilation of data on out-of-hospital birth from various state health departments. Of the eleven states which had statistics ready at that time, all showed a two- to five-times-higher risk of infant loss associated with out-of-hospital delivery. In 1977, in the state of California alone, 79 home-delivered babies died who would not have died in hospitals. California also reported 25 stillbirths per 1000 births for out-of-hospital deliveries, as compared with 9.9 stillbirths per 1000 hospital births.

A more recent report from the New York State Department of Health reviewed statistics on home births for the years 1973–76 in all of New York outside New York City. The figures showed the neonatal mortality rate overall to be 37 per 1000 in the home setting as compared to 11 per 1000 in hospitals. Furthermore, in a presumably low-risk population of white mothers who began prenatal care in the first trimester of pregnancy, the neonatal mortality rate was 39.3 per 1000 in the home, as compared to 8.7 per 1000 in hospitals.

"We can complain with some justification about the lack of spirituality associated with birth and death in modern society," says David Kliot, "but when we talk about making childbirth more humane, we can forget 'the good old days,' because they never existed. Childbirth has always been associated with pain and extreme risk. It is only now, in the twentieth century, that scientific achievements in obstetrics have allowed us the luxury of contemplating how childbirth might be accomplished without unnecessary trauma to either mother or newborn."

Obstetricians are not ogres. Yes, certainly there is some concern about the damage a flourishing home birth movement might do to the physician's pocketbook; this is normal. But I believe that most of the opposition to out-of-hospital birth is founded on the sincere conviction that it is overly risky. Doctors who go into the business of delivering babies do it because they like it; they want those babies, and their mothers, to survive.

Does it necessarily follow that twentieth-century expectant parents ought to accept meekly the type of regimented, impersonal maternity care previously described? Not at all. Alternatives are available today, and their numbers are increasing. Our job, as educated consumers, is to choose wisely among them.

The family-centered maternity unit. One of the major advantages of living in a free enterprise economy is that consumer selection frequently (although certainly not invariably) weeds out the bad apples in the bushel. The achievement of family-centered obstetrical care within the hospital setting needn't, therefore, be looked upon as a utopian dream.

During the past few years, combined pressure from women's groups (i.e., the consumers of maternity health care) and reformers within the obstetrical establishment has scored major victories and effected substantial changes in areas once thought to be unassailable. The admission of fathers to the delivery room, even to the operating room for routine cesarean section, was one such victory. Rooming-in of newborns and, more recently, sibling visitation during the postpartum period were others. The endorsement of a document favoring family-centered maternity/newborn care* by the American College of Obstetricians and Gynecologists, while perhaps a bow to the inevitable, at least indicates considerable professional interest in this healthy trend.

And there are other tangible indications of progress. We have already discussed the importance to gentle birth of having a caring, supportive person remain with the woman in labor to monitor fetal heart rate and uterine contractions, extend reassurance to the couple, and oversee the birth of their child. Where this need is not being met by physicians, a growing body of highly trained certified nurse-midwives (RNs who have completed postgraduate training and obtained certification from the American College of Nurse-Midwives) are stepping in to fill the role. The "team" approach to obstetrics—in which a midwife provides prenatal care and manages the bulk of uncomplicated deliveries, backed up by a physician who takes over when operative procedures are called for—has proved to be a very effective arrangement in normal births.

* See page 149.

Birthing room, White Plains (New York) Hospital [Used by permission]

Another encouraging sign has been the setting up, within some large hospitals, of multipurpose labor/delivery/recovery rooms, or "birthing" suites, in which an entire childbirth experience, from early labor through recovery, can take place in comfort and privacy without the woman ever having to set foot in an operating room. "It's an obvious absurdity," Kliot points out. "We take a patient at the height of her discomfort, disconnect her from the monitors, move her down the hall onto another bed, and achieve nothing except additional anxiety for the woman and her husband and the dirtying of another set of linen."

Some birthing rooms are quite glamorously decorated, with comfy sofas and adjacent kitchenettes, the requisite equipment cleverly camouflaged behind attractive wall coverings, paintings, and green plants. But decor is far less important than the atmosphere created by this simple change in environment. Mr. and Mrs. H. express the reaction of many couples: "Staying in one room for labor and delivery was very important to us, because in a few hours we had become familiar with it and could regard it as 'our' bedroom, so there was nothing to jar our concentration."

A step above the birthing suite is the family-centered maternity center, or hospital. Also called alternative birth centers, these are small, private institutions completely dedicated to the principles of family care. There are not many in the United States at the present time, and they vary considerably with regard to staffing and quality of care. One of the most effective, in view of the broad scope of its programs and incorporation of a full range of hospital safety features, is the Booth Maternity Center in Philadelphia.

Opened on July 1, 1971, Booth is a Salvation Army hospital geared to meet the needs of both indigent pregnant adolescents and ordinary low-to-moderate-risk pregnant women interested in this approach. Patients are carefully screened prior to admission, and women with special problems are automatically referred elsewhere—as happens in other countries with "two-phase" obstetrical systems, such as the Netherlands and Denmark. The center has pediatricians on staff and anesthesia service on call, and is equipped to handle cesarean birth and uncomplicated prematurity. In case of emergency, mother and child are removed by ambulance to Thomas Jefferson Medical College Hospital, Booth's "backup," for more aggressive treatment.

Because of its shoestring budget, Booth cannot afford plush carpeting or designer graphics. "Instead," says its director, John Franklin, M.D., "we concentrate on an atmosphere of personalized care, and making the expectant mother feel that she has primary responsibility for the manner in which she gives birth."

At the first prenatal visit, all Booth parents are encouraged to select, from the chart shown of alternative possibilities, the kind of childbirth experience they feel would be most suitable for *them.* Included are such issues as use of medication, choice of support person(s), gentle or "quiet" birth, breast or bottle feeding, and sibling visitation.

In later visits for checkups and childbirth education classes, the couple have a chance to become acquainted with the physical setup, learn about hospital procedures, and get to know the doctors and midwives long before they are scheduled for admission. After the birth, far from losing contact with the center, many couples return as "Booth buddies" to offer moral support and firsthand advice on baby care to other new parents.

The Salvation Army
Booth Maternity Center
6051 Overbrook Avenue
Philadelphia, Pa. 19131

GOAL SHEET

MR-5 3-77

Why did you choose Booth for your birth experience?

How did you hear about Booth?

What is especially important to you in this birth experience?

PRENATAL	INITIAL PLAN	36 WEEKS
Classes — Previous class		
— Plan to attend		
— Orientation		
— Prep. Childbirth - 6 wks.		
— Labor Prep. - 2 wks.		
— Other		
Infant Feeding		
— Breast		
— Bottle		
— Unsure		
Special Needs		

CHILDBIRTH	INITIAL PLAN	36 WEEKS
Support Person		
Type of Birth Desired		
— CCB/Minimal meds.		
— Quiet birth		
— Medication		
— Medication discussed		
☐ Demerol		
☐ Epidural		
☐ Paracervical		
☐ Pudendal/Local		
Special Needs (e.g. bed birth, no episiotomy, etc.)		

AFTER BABY IS BORN	GOING HOME
— Length of stay	— Help at home
— Special diet	— Doctor for baby
— Circumcision	— Supplies
— Sibling visit	— VNA
— Family planning	— Nursing Mothers
— Tubal ligation	— Parenting Group
Special Needs	Special Needs

Midwives provide primary and continuous care for all Booth patients, although an obstetrician is present in the building during deliveries to take over if there is a problem or simply to provide an extra pair of hands, should the midwife request it.

"The physician, who has been trained to sense danger wherever he looks, finds himself automatically calling for the monitors and starting an I.V.," notes Franklin. "The atmosphere is tense, waiting. By contrast, the midwife can say, 'Okay, honey, it's time to

93

have your baby,' and immediately the mood shifts, the woman gains confidence."

In such a supportive setting, the need for anesthesia drops sharply. Current statistics at Booth show that, barring the small percentage who require cesareans, only 30 percent of first-time mothers request an epidural block, in contrast to the 60 percent to 70 percent of first-time mothers given anesthesia at neighboring, larger institutions. As a consequence, the incidence of such surgical interventions as forceps delivery and episiotomy is markedly low.

Uncomplicated deliveries may take place in the labor or delivery rooms, and women are given free choice of delivery position. (As anyone who has ever tried to use a hospital bedpan knows, it's nearly impossible to push effectively lying flat on your back. The traditional supine or "lithotomy" position is not only a very inefficient and uncomfortable way in which to give birth, it is also medically undesirable, because uterine pressure on the vena cava causes a drop in the mother's blood pressure which potentially reduces the baby's oxygen supply.) Knowing that it is in their own interest that the midwife or doctor see what is going on, prepared Booth mothers invariably select very sensible delivery positions: semisitting against a backrest or side-lying (Sims' position).

The atmosphere throughout is very quiet and low-key. At birth the infant is placed directly on the mother's abdomen, suctioned or not, as necessary, and covered with a warm blanket. The cord is left intact until it has stopped pulsating, and administration of eyedrops is delayed for about three hours, so as not to interfere with the baby's ability to "track."

The newborn is examined in front of the parents by the nurse midwife and later by a pediatrician. Both parents are offered refreshment, and the mother is given any help she needs in encouraging the baby to nurse. For the duration of the hospital stay, mother, father, and baby continue to be cared for as a unit. Each mother has twenty-four-hour access to her infant, so that she can adjust feedings to conform to their particular rhythms.

With the accumulated experience of over five thousand births since its opening and no shortage of satisfied parents to act as "buddies," Booth Maternity Center is what family-centered care is all about.

AWAKE, AWARE, AND ELATED

Establishment of synchrony depends upon having two partners who are capable of responding to one another. Without a certain level of awareness in both mother and infant, the exchange of signals that forms the basis of communication cannot take place. Klaus and Kennell note:

In our own experience we have been amazed at the differences between large numbers of infants born in other countries with no maternal analgesia or anesthesia and the neonates in the United States delivered under minimal analgesia and conduction anesthesia. The latter infants need to be treated as postsurgical (or postanesthesia) patients for many hours, with head positioned low, repeated suctioning, and close watching . . .
. . . The relief of pain for a short period of time has to be weighed against the effects of altering this unique experience in the life of a woman, which under unmodified conditions, is reported to be frequently associated with orgasmic sensations and followed by a period of particularly heightened perceptions. In contrast are the sometimes hectic, painful, and awkward maneuvers needed to administer conduction anesthesia as labor progresses rapidly; the relatively common postspinal headaches that keep mothers lying on their backs and limit interaction with their infants for three to five days; and the effects of episiotomy repairs on the comfort, mobility, and ability of the mother to care for her baby. These negative factors must be balanced against the relatively brief period of intense pain associated with natural childbirth.[1]

How painful *is* childbirth? Overwhelming evidence indicates that the only correct answer is: that depends. Although first deliveries are generally hardest, many women breeze through their first, only to encounter unexpected difficulties with number two or three. In each instance, the relationship of the infant's head to the mother's pelvis (cephalopelvic ratio) will differ. Furthermore, response to pain is highly individual: there are considerable variations in both the number of pain messages reaching the brain and the degree to which their perception may be altered by psychological factors.

It is generally believed that for a small percentage of women (say, 5 percent), childbirth is totally pain-free. For the rest of us, what we stand to gain from Lamaze or other training will depend to a large degree upon our general suggestibility, the amount of support we receive from our labor coach or coaches, and the type of environment we choose for giving birth.

"I have persistently called attention to the desperate loneliness of the unattended woman in labor," says John Grover. Indeed, it should be obvious at this point that a sympathetic maternity setting and a close and trusting relationship with those who are present can make an enormous difference in a woman's perception of her childbirth experience.

There used to be a school of thought that held that childbirth had actually become more difficult, because modern women had lost the "natural" abilities of their hunter-gatherer ancestors for giving birth. While it is a fact that squatting (whether behind a clump of brush or on a labor bed) is probably a more productive position for expelling a baby than lying flat on one's back, anthropologic investigation by Margaret Mead and others indicates that childbirth has *never* been regarded lightly, but rather has— throughout history—been seen as unpleasant, painful, or fraught with supernatural hazards depending upon the particular cultural patterns of the society involved. In areas where the couvade is still practiced, a laboring woman's husband may moan and cry out with anguish equaling, or even exceeding, that of his wife. Use of drugs and stimulation of labor by various techniques aimed at encouraging oxytocin release are likewise not limited to Western obstetrical practice.

What *was* undeniable was that the atmosphere of fear engendered by repetition of old wives' tales and the strapping down of hysterical women in labor, in the absence of any real knowledge about childbearing, had contributed to the setting-up of what Grantly Dick-Read termed a "fear-tension-pain" syndrome.

Read's *Childbirth Without Fear* (4th ed., 1972) cited the studies of Russian physiologist Ivan Pavlov on conditioned behavior in dogs and humans, and suggested steps for "deconditioning" pregnant women away from such negative stimuli. By educating women for birth, removing destructive images from the terminology (for example, substitution of the word "contraction" for "pain"), encouraging the participation of fathers, and teaching mastery of relaxation and breathing exercises to combat discomfort, Read hoped to restore childbirth to its natural, spiritual—and also, presumably, pain-free—state.

As applied by later Soviet scientists to the mystery of labor pain, Pavlovian conditioning took the form of "psychoprophylaxis," or mental blocking of unpleasant sensations through intense concentration on breath control and simultaneous relaxation of the pelvic muscles. After traveling to Russia in the early 1950s, French obstetrician Fernand Lamaze decided that Frenchwomen, too, could benefit from the techniques and incorporated them into his Paris trade union clinic. Under his leadership and that of another, like-minded obstetrician, Pierre Vellay, the "Lamaze" movement spread rapidly through Europe and then America.

It was found that women who had been educated for giving birth could endure the discomfort of labor with far less medication and required fewer surgical interventions at the time of delivery. Recent studies also suggest that Lamaze-prepared patients have fewer obstetrical complications and deliver healthier babies than unprepared women.

Before we review the evidence in its favor, however, two things about psychoprophylaxis deserve emphasis: First, it can hardly be called "natural" childbirth, inasmuch as success depends upon the woman's acquisition of a set of totally artificial conditioned responses. Second, it doesn't work for everybody.

Medical evidence. Scientific concern about the effects of obstetrical anesthesia on the newborn grew out of the gradual realization that the placenta is far from the barrier it was once thought to be. In fact, nearly all of the drugs administered to pregnant women —nausea remedies, cold pills, analgesics, regional and general anesthetics—rapidly cross the placental membrane and enter the fetal circulation. Because the baby's organs of elimination are not yet fully developed, it takes longer for potentially dangerous chemicals to be cleared, with the result that any given dosage of medication will be that much more potent.

Numerous studies have observed that infants born to sedated mothers tend to be sluggish and unresponsive in comparison with infants born to unmedicated mothers. Inhibition of the sucking reflex is another frequently cited finding. Most serious of all is the threat of respiratory depression, which can occur regardless of the mode of drug administration and may be associated with

long-range neurobehavioral consequences that remain undetected until the child reaches school age. "We know that even
minimal doses of Demerol will have some effect on the fetal respiratory center," affirms William Gottschalk, M.D., who teaches
obstetric anesthesiology at Chicago's Rush Medical College.
"While these changes may play no role whatsoever in the case of
an otherwise healthy infant, we have no idea of their effect on
newborns already at risk of other problems—particularly respiratory distress syndrome."

Further complicating this issue, says Dr. Gottschalk, is the fact
that narcotics are frequently *misused* in obstetrics. Often they are
begun too early—for example, to calm anxiety in the poorly educated patient. Rather than being given some verbal encouragement or maybe a mild tranquilizer, the woman is started on a
narcotic agent even before she is actually in pain.

The apparently lower incidence of respiratory distress syndrome in babies born to unmedicated mothers prompted researchers to undertake closer examination of Lamaze-prepared
women, to see if there might be additional benefits accruing from
the technique. In a 1975–76 study in Evanston, Illinois, five
hundred Lamaze-trained pregnant women were compared with
a hand-picked (that is, matched by age, race, number of previous pregnancies, and educational level) control group of five
hundred pregnant women not prepared by this method. "In
virtually every obstetric performance category," the investigators
reported, "these data suggest that the Lamaze method is beneficial."[2]

Lamaze-prepared women had almost twice the number of
spontaneous deliveries and only one-fourth the number of cesarean sections as women in the control group. The incidence of
fetal distress (see chart) was one-fifth, and perinatal mortality was
one-fourth. Lamaze babies also scored better on both one- and
five-minute Apgar evaluations.

Among the mothers, the rate of postpartum infection was one-
third in the Lamaze group. There were fewer perineal lacera-
tions, and those that occurred were less serious than those occur-
ring in control patients. A most surprising finding was that
unprepared mothers had almost three times the incidence of
pregnancy-induced hypertension and twice as many premature
births as Lamaze-prepared women.

"It makes little difference how stressful a woman's childbirth experience has been," says John Grover, "I can ask her thirty seconds after I've put that baby on her stomach how she feels, and the answer will always come back, 'Wonderful.' " Prepared childbirth and gentle handling of the newborn work hand in hand, the one encouraging the other: "There comes a moment during almost any labor—often during the 'transition' phase—when a woman will say to her husband or her doctor, 'I can't stand this anymore.' She may not actually be in great pain, but there is a feeling of panic that comes over a woman in labor who knows she isn't supposed to push yet, but feels her body going out of control . . . Or perhaps labor has been very long and the woman simply feels too exhausted to give that long, final push that will expel the baby. Whatever the reason, when that moment comes, if her labor coach can gently remind her that in another minute or two all the commotion will have ceased and she will be hugging her baby and calling him by name, she generally will summon the strength to get through, without extra medication."

INDICATIONS* FOR CESAREAN SECTION IN LAMAZE-PREPARED (LP) PATIENTS AND MATCHED CONTROLS

	Number of patients	
Indication	*LP*	*Control*
Cephalopelvic disproportion	12	21
Breech	3	12
Fetal distress	3	16
Inertia	1	2
Placenta previa	—	4
Toxemia of pregnancy	—	4
Transverse lie	—	1
Prolapsed cord	—	1
Abruptio placentae	—	1
Prolonged rupture of membranes	—	3
Postdatism	—	1
Failure to progress in labor	—	4
TOTAL	16	60

SOURCE; M. J. Hughey, T. W. McElin, and T. Young, "Maternal and Fetal Outcome of Lamaze-Prepared Patients," *Obstetrics and Gynecology*, June 1978. Used by permission.
* Some patients had multiple indications.

Fifteen years ago, Grover notes, his response to the same situation would have been to slip in a spinal and deliver the baby with forceps. Since then his experience with Lamaze-prepared patients has convinced him of the value of trying "verbal anesthesia" first.

Gentle birth with a regional block. Taken in proper perspective, Lamaze training can be enormously valuable for the expectant couple. Not only is the medical evidence in favor of unmedicated birth impressive, but the psychological advantages of preparedness—in sweeping away the fears that paralyzed our mothers and grandmothers, bringing husband and wife closer together prior to the birth event, providing peer support during this generally traumatic period, and encouraging a level of consciousness sufficient to promote maternal-infant attachment—appear, certainly at first glance, to be limitless.

The trouble is that, misapplied, the concept of "natural" childbirth easily becomes a tyrant, dooming to unnecessary feelings of failure and disappointment those well-intentioned parents who, for any of a dozen reasons, find that the breathing and relaxation techniques simply don't work for them. And at the very moment when they ought to have everything in the world to cheer about!

Psychoprophylaxis may be the best of a number of alternatives for helping women through childbirth, but it is hardly a religion. Some women are constitutionally unsuited to psychological conditioning, just as others may be inappropriate candidates for other forms of anesthesia. And (let's face it), some labors are just longer, and harder, and more frustrating than others. In view of the fact that primitive women felt free to avail themselves of the potions brewed by the tribal shaman, it seems absurd to think that in our present culture, childbirth should become an endurance test for the mother's ability to withstand pain.

Furthermore, not all drugs used in labor are equally dangerous to the fetus. There are, for example, differences in the makeup of various agents used in local anesthesia that may have real significance in terms of newborn responsiveness. A drug that only crosses the placenta in small quantities, or is so readily detoxified that the baby actually receives very little is obviously preferable to an agent that possesses neither of these qualities. Since every physician has particular preferences regarding medication, it is wise —even if you are planning on unmedicated labor and delivery— to have a talk with your doctor about possible alternatives prior to hospital admission.

One of the nicest things about having a family-centered setting for birth is that the laboring woman knows that any decision to use drugs will be arrived at collectively, and not out of force of habit on the physician's part or apparent conspiracy on the part of the obstetrical team. (At one time it was considered routine hospital practice to give 200 milligrams of oral Seconal on admission to the maternity unit, followed by an injection of scopolamine and Demerol—in many cases before the woman's physician had even arrived to examine her!)

In addition, although the unanesthetized patient has a clear advantage when it comes to knowing when and how hard to push, the incidence of forceps delivery with epidural medication is considerably lessened when there is a trusted professional—whether monitrice, midwife, or M.D.—around to coach the mother to bear down at the proper time.

As we have noted already, verbal support is frequently enough to carry a woman through a crisis period. However, as valuable as childbirth education is per se,* expectant couples should guard against accepting easy generalities, regardless of the source. A woman who is completely exhausted and numb from an overlong and uncomfortable labor may find it just as difficult to respond to her baby's signals as an overmedicated mother. Certainly, acceptance of a short-acting synthetic narcotic such as Nisentil, epidural anesthesia for pelvic delivery, or even a spinal for cesarean section does not preclude a woman from fully enjoying a family-centered nonviolent birth.

Gentle birth and cesarean section. One situation in which some form of anesthesia is unavoidable is cesarean section. Where medical indications call for a general anesthetic, immediate postpartum contact is obviously an impossibility. But cesarean section with regional anesthesia lends itself very well to the gentle birth approach.

Although the incision site must be well-lit, the baby's eyes can be shielded until he is placed upon his mother's thighs—the abdomen cannot, obviously, be used because of the danger of contamination of the wound. After a pause of a moment or two, the cord is divided and the baby's pharynx sucked out. (Contractions of the birth canal during pelvic delivery squeeze much of the mucus out of the newborn's mouth, pharynx, and lungs. Cesarean babies, who do not have the advantage of this "thoracic squeeze," generally require some aspiration, even in gentle births.)

---

* And the classes may be particularly valuable in the case of gentle birth, to give the parents-to-be a sense of confidence in handling the baby and prepare them for what he will actually feel like (that is, warm and sticky) as opposed to what they may expect. There is also a considerable amount of deprogramming involved, in that we have all been conditioned to accept a crying infant as a healthy one.

Following a brief examination by the pediatrician, the infant is given to his father for the bath. During this period, the mother is generally close enough to stroke the baby with her free hand and feel him respond to her touch. After the bath, the baby is wrapped in a warm blanket and placed in his father's arms, yet close enough to the mother that she, too, has direct visual contact with him. Father and newborn then retire briefly, while the incision is closed. Finally, the family is reunited in the recovery room, where the mother has her first opportunity to cuddle the infant and place him at her breast to nurse. Postpartum arrangements, including rooming-in, can be the same as they would be following vaginal delivery, unless the parents request otherwise.

By making allowances for the operative procedure in this fashion, yet preserving the basic elements of family-centered care, gentle childbirth works to reduce the feelings of disappointment and frustration acknowledged by many couples in the past after a cesarean birth experience.*

SUBDUED ENVIRONMENT

Animal species, whether wild or domesticated, ordinarily seek out dark, secluded areas for giving birth. The mother baboon who isolates herself in a dark cave, the house cat hiding in the linen closet or dresser drawer, the formerly gentle bitch who snarls when anyone dares approach her pups—all are displaying innate patterns of behavior which, over the course of thousands of years, have proved their suitability for the protection of the fragile young.

Even Homo sapiens—removed as we are from our roots in the wild—remains linked to other primate species in our choice of a time to be born. During the 1960s, a study was made of over six hundred thousand spontaneous deliveries, which showed a peak of births between 3:00 and 4:00 A.M., when the mother was most

---

* In addition to the sense of estrangement felt by ordinary parents who are denied extended contact, cesarean mothers often worry that their bodies have "failed" to perform normally—that they are, somehow, less than complete women. In the absence of a strongly positive postpartum experience such as the one just described, the longer hospital stay, increased immobilization, fatigue, and, for most women, realization that they are likely to repeat the process with each subsequent birth may contribute to a whopping case of the "baby blues."

likely to be in a quiet, darkened environment, away from disturb-ing interruptions.

Of course, the genetic program could hardly be expected to take into account the modern, institutional setting for birth with its instrument clatter and overpowering brightness!

"We maintain a very quiet, low-key and low-lit atmosphere," says midwife Ruth Wilf of the Booth Maternity Center.[3] Why do the practitioners of family-centered care—and those who special-ize in gentle birth in particular—insist upon a subdued atmo-sphere for labor and delivery? Because it is as safe as the two-thousand-watt delivery room setting, for one thing. Because the parents feel more comfortable in an atmosphere that takes their need for privacy into consideration, for another. But primarily because study after study has shown that *babies don't like* bright lights and loud, unfamiliar noises. And newborn babies who are involved in crying and turning inward cannot also be involved in taking in their surroundings and gazing at their parents.

John Grover recalls being startled the first time he saw a baby open its eyes after birth—and keep them open. A nurse had shown him that simply shading the infant's face with the palm of her hand would cause the eyes to open much wider than was customarily seen following delivery. "Of course," Grover adds, "babies often do open their eyes for brief periods during conven-tional births as well, but the relaxed manner in which they con-tinue to gaze about them in a darkened room is something quite different."

To recap: The delivery area is never completely black during gentle birth; there is always sufficient illumination to observe the mother's condition and determine whether the baby is sluggish in any way or having difficulty breathing. And in the event anes-thesia or a surgical procedure is called for, adequate lighting is provided for that. But no more. Nothing unnecessary that would detract from the peacefulness of the tableau of baby and parents meeting for the first time.

The parents speak for themselves:

"I was absolutely hypnotized . . ."

"A very, very moving experience . . ."

"The delivery room was so hushed and calm I didn't even worry about doing my breathing properly. I just kept talking to my husband, between pants, and pushed when the doctor said to. And out she came. There was absolutely no question in either of our minds that *this was our baby.*"

DELAYED CORD CLAMPING

When a newborn infant makes her entrance into the world, breathing begins naturally. With the first expansion of the chest, air enters the baby's nose and throat. As the lungs expand to accommodate it, the fluid that earlier filled the pulmonary alveoli is absorbed into the blood and lymphatic circulation.

Whether this transition is gradual or abrupt depends upon a single factor: the timing of the cutting of the umbilical cord. Leboyer contends:

If the cord is severed as soon as the baby is born, this brutally deprives the brain of oxygen.
The alarm system thus alerted, the baby's entire organism reacts. Respiration is thrown into high gear as a response to aggression.[4]

There are, of course, emergency situations in which the cord must be clamped and severed immediately so that lifesaving procedures may be instituted. But these are very, very rare. For the most part, the cord is cut immediately in normal deliveries so that the baby can be removed from the mother and medical routines initiated.

Leboyer correctly noted that allowing the baby to set the tempo after delivery would be hard for the overeager Western mind to accept. "*Everything,*" he wrote, "inclines us to act; our mental laziness, our automatic assumptions, our habits. And our everlasting impatience."[5]

And yet delaying the moment of detachment from the placenta is enormously logical from a strictly medical standpoint. For as long as the cord is intact, the baby is receiving oxygen from two sources: oxygenated blood from her mother's circulation and her own gradually clearing respiratory system. Nature, Leboyer pointed out, has wisely provided this dual shelter from the dangers of anoxia, brain damage, and death. It is man who misunderstands, who slaps the newborn to hear confirmation of the baby's panic and then proceeds to justify that panic by forcing the infant to breathe on her own before she is ready . . . to run, in a sense, before she can walk.

Original critics of the method voiced some concern about the possibility of anemia, claiming that the pull of gravity would cause significant amounts of the infant's blood to transfuse back into the placenta, as the baby lay on the mother's abdomen. However, none of the investigations of Leboyer babies has shown any evidence of this, even when the cord is cut a full ten minutes after birth. As long as the placenta remains attached, normal postpartum uterine contractions effectively squeeze placental blood into the infant.

The only certain results of late cord clamping have been that (1) the newborn makes the transition to respiration without having to draw in deep gasps of air; and (2) the mother has an extra five minutes or so in which to accept that her discomfort is over and this infant, still physically linked to her body, is now a separate individual.

SKIN TO SKIN

Safely breathing, the baby needs time to rest and to discover that even though the womb has ejected him, there is still comfort in his world. Your belly, soft and slack now, forms an ideal cradle. On it, he can be almost as comfortable as he was in it. There he can rest.[6]

The ability of a mother's touch—and, above all, the sound of her heartbeat—to soothe a frightened, agitated infant has been shown beyond the shadow of a doubt in repeated experiments. (As though this fact, which has been understood by mothers since time immemorial, needed additional scientific demonstration!) Yet infants delivered in traditional hospital surroundings experience little body contact with their mothers after birth and have almost no opportunity to hear the beloved, familiar sound.

As for the mother herself, Grover comments: "I have philosophically given a great deal of thought to helping the mother deal with her sense of physical loss as the baby is born. Her reaching down and touching the baby as it is coming out, and actually helping to bring it onto her stomach, seems to matter a great deal in many cases. But probably more important is the subsequent skin-to-skin contact with the wet, squirmy infant. It is surprising that more has not been written about this phenomenon. How could a woman who has carried a fetus inside herself for over nine months *not* feel a sense of loss when it physically leaves her body?"

In an ordinary delivery, the cord is clamped immediately and the infant held upside down briefly by the obstetrician. Then the nurse places the baby on his back—a very contrary position, in that the force of gravity will propel any material blocking the tracheopharyngeal tree directly downward into the lungs. (It's rather like putting a drowning person on his back, rather than his stomach.)

The original rationale for placing the baby on his back was to ease the introduction of a catheter, which might be required in addition to the routine bulb syringe for sucking out nasopharyngeal mucus so that the baby would not breathe it in. This was clearly Catch-22 reasoning, since it was the use of the supine position which made some inhalation of liquid by the gasping, "drowning" infant almost inevitable!

Nature's way is, once again, more effective. Simply placing the newborn face down in a so-called postural drainage position (see chart) eliminates the need for additional suctioning in most cases. The changeover from "wet" lung to "dry" lung is accomplished without additional trauma and without the danger of an anoxic episode—which can be the result of too-vigorous mechanical suction and subsequent spasm of the vocal chords.

Courtesy of David Kliot, M.D.

TRADITIONAL
DELIVERY
POSITION

VS.

POSTURAL
DRAINAGE
POSITION

Placing the infant skin to skin against the mother's abdomen in no way interferes with the physician's ability to monitor the baby's responses. The heart rate is easily checked by stethoscope, a hand slipped beneath the baby's chest, or feeling the cord pulse. Furthermore, it is believed that the natural rocking motion created by the mother's rhythmical breathing may actually be a useful built-in mechanism for assisting onset of respiration.

While Leboyer's original recommendation that the customary sterile drape between mother and baby be eliminated was met with horror—and the certainty that this would be an invitation to infection in the newborn—the reverse has proved true. Not only is direct skin contact emotionally gratifying to mothers and babies, it is probably protective as well, in that the baby's early acquisition of strains of his mother's respiratory organisms appears to provide "bacterial interference" against more pathologic organisms that abound in hospitals.

"We have no reason for assuming that the bacterial flora of the mother's abdomen will be any more harmful to the baby on the first day of life than it will be a day or two later," notes Kliot. The mother's abdomen may be prepped with sterile solution or un-prepped with absolutely no difference in newborn infection rates.*

Another early fear was hypothermia—a sudden drop in body temperature that could be deadly to a newborn baby with under-developed thermoregulatory mechanisms. Newborn temperatures normally drop one or two degrees after birth; would the drop be precipitous if babies were allowed to remain with their mothers, as opposed to being immediately placed in incubators?

But the fear of "cold stress," too, proved to be unfounded. The mother's abdomen provides a natural source of radiant heat, and a light blanket over the baby's back is more than sufficient for normal room temperatures, even with air conditioning. Although some obstetricians prefer to dry the babies gently as they emerge, wet skin is at least as good a heat transfer medium—and, Grover comments, "a human being's first contact with the world ought to be with another human being . . . not a linen towel!"

The babies are *always* dried thoroughly after the bath, then wrapped warmly. "I could go into the nursery any day," says Grover, "and compare the temperatures of all of the incoming babies for that day, and the gentle birth babies will almost invariably be two or three degrees warmer."

---

* There is a necessity for overcautiousness in trying any new medical technique. Like the use of sterile water for the first Leboyer baths, prepping the mother's abdomen for reception of the baby is being gradually discontinued as the safety of immediate skin contact is recognized.

One young mother whose infant was delivered by modified Leboyer techniques recalls: "My pediatrician objected to the danger of the baby losing heat while on my stomach, so I was particularly careful to keep her close to me and cover us both with warm sheets. As a result, the only time she felt cool in those first hours was after she had been in the nursery for about twenty minutes for the examination. Of course, after that I just cuddled her close to me again!"

BABY MASSAGE

The massaging of newborn infants by their parents and birth attendants was, Leboyer knew, commonplace in other cultures. With the aid of local materials ranging from coconut oil to cow dung, Asian, African, and Indian mothers have for centuries practiced this simple art, which encourages early motor development while at the same time providing soothing tactile stimulation.

Massaging down baby's arm

Massaging down baby's back

There is no mystique surrounding the massage, other than the fact that it takes a little practice (generally learned as part of childbirth education class) for parents to learn to be both gentle and decisive in their movements. New parents are inclined to be nervous and hesitant in handling their babies at first, and the infants, sensing this, tend to become jittery themselves.

The baby is gently stroked, using the flat of the hand to provide firm, rhythmic movement, first along the back toward the buttocks, then down the arms and legs. (See illustrations.) The white, creamy vernix provides natural lubrication.

That a being who appears so tiny and frail actually welcomes the steady pressure of his parents' hands is understandable when one recalls that just before birth the fetus is actually very tightly confined. Supported on all sides by amniotic fluid and the sturdy walls of his mother's womb, rocked by her swaying body movements, he naturally expects to find more of the same in the extrauterine world.

Small wonder that researchers are beginning to take a second look at the contentment of children in those cultures where it is customary for infants to remain "in arms" from birth until toddlerhood. Or that soft cloth baby carriers, modeled after those traditionally worn by tribal women to free their arms for other tasks, are currently in vogue among busy Western mothers. Small wonder, too, that babies show such a marked preference for enclosed spaces—a cradle, car bed, or dresser drawer, as opposed to the standard oversized crib—or that if placed in the center of such a crib overnight, they will migrate . . . and be found by a surprised parent the next morning, with their heads wedged tightly into one of the corners!

Besides fulfilling the newborn's need for encirclement and contact comfort, the massage also serves a second function. This is to introduce the particular contours and anatomical features of *this* baby to his parents. Having accepted him as an individual, they can begin to love him as one. The gentle, rhythmical touch of loving hands, says Leboyer, speaks in a language that is both timeless and universal.

WATER BATH

Of all of Leboyer's departures from standard obstetrical procedure, the bath has been by far the most controversial. Even those physicians who felt drawn to the idea of gentleness in childbirth were at first reluctant to allow the babies to be immersed in water. Their reasoning was threefold: first, fear of cold stress, such as we have described; second, fear of infection from organisms lurking in the bathwater; third, fear that the nervous father would inadvertently drop the infant or submerge the head for long enough to drown the baby.

The last, completely exaggerated concern illustrates the widespread medical conviction—shared, unfortunately, by many new parents—that mothers and fathers are inappropriate caretakers for fragile newborns. It is no more likely that the baby will drown in the tub on the first day of life than after discharge from the hospital (when, it is assumed, the parents will be in charge of bathing).

Furthermore, no one, Leboyer least of all, ever suggested that the father immerse the baby without adequate guidance. In fact,

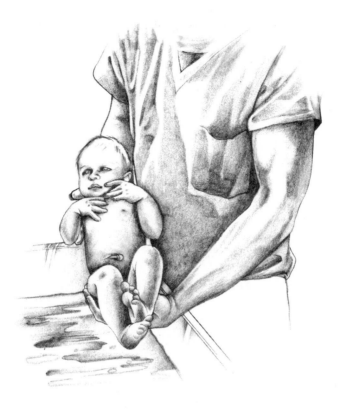

Lowering baby into bath—shoulders, neck, buttocks supported

all baths in gentle birth are closely assisted by the obstetrician or midwife in charge. Once the baby has been gently lowered into the water (see illustration), the father simply cradles the newborn's head between his hands to prevent the baby from submerging her face as she moves about. The legs are left free to splash and explore.

The temperature of the bathwater is easily checked by thermometer or an experienced wrist or elbow. If the baby is promptly dried afterward, snugly dressed, and returned to her mother's arms, there is no danger of cold stress.

Some hospitals place the tub beneath a radiant heater as a precautionary measure. Although this certainly is not harmful, it is not necessary provided the depth of the water is adequate to cover the baby's torso. *Nobody* likes to take a bath in just an inch or two of water!

As for the threat of infection, this simply did not materialize. Whether the water used for bathing was presterilized or from the nearest tap appeared to have absolutely no effect on the infants' susceptibility to pathogenic bacteria. Insofar as their infection rates were concerned, gentle birth babies were unremarkable.

What was remarkable, as anyone who witnessed the early bathing sequences was quick to point out, was the behavior of the infants in this new situation and the response of parents and other, presumably less biased, observers. Comments David Kliot: "Within a few seconds of being immersed in the bath, the baby usually develops a very alert, responsive state that has no relation to the 'startling' response to unpleasant stimuli. The infant moves her arms about gracefully. Controlled head movements are apparent. The baby's gaze is clearly seen to shift in response to her mother's or father's voice. Trained observers who are watching a gentle delivery for the first time often remark that the newborn 'acts like a three-week-old.'. . ."

Some infants appear serious, others, quite comical. Many babies stick their tongues out—which invariably brings a laugh of delight from the parents.

While all of this is going on, the obstetrician has a chance to make a much more detailed assessment of newborn capabilities than is possible during the brief period generally reserved for Apgar scoring. And the parents are given time to gradually adjust any earlier expectations they have formed to match the appearance of the infant they see before them.

This is a well-documented process that takes place whenever a child is born. During pregnancy, all couples enjoy fantasizing about how their offspring will look and behave. For the relationship to start off well it is critical that any alterations in this mental picture be made as quickly as possible.

With the majority of healthy babies this happens semiautomatically. (Remember the pull of the infant's vulnerable appearance and the powerful biological mechanisms encouraging maternal-infant attachment.) But there are exceptions. The pro-football coach who was looking forward to a team of his own and already has two daughters may not be especially thrilled to hear that he now has a third—if the news arrives in the form of a congratulatory word or two delivered in the waiting room.

If, on the other hand, the same father is allowed to assist in the birth and then encouraged to interact separately with the infant during the bath, his response may be quite different. What begins as a casual suggestion from the obstetrician to "just hold her for a minute . . . like this . . . see, she won't break," is likely to end with the father noticing that this baby already responds to his voice, marveling at what a strong grip she has, and remarking to all within earshot that "women have terrific opportunities in sports nowadays!"

For new mothers, the bath represents a chance to exchange roles with their husbands, momentarily giving up the primary responsibility for caretaking in return for the sheer pleasure of watching the baby discover her arms and legs for the first time. Says one mother going back for her second gentle birth, reminiscing about the first: "In the beginning, I was so overcome by what was happening that when my little girl was placed on my abdomen I couldn't focus on her. When my husband held her in the bath, I guess I felt I could relax for a while, and that's when I really began to watch her."

After the exhaustion of labor and childbirth, most women welcome the respite offered by the bath as a chance to catch their breath, take stock, and get their first good look at the new arrival. (Although the outlines of the baby's head and body are clearly visible while the infant is on the abdomen, the first maternal contact is still basically one of touch.)

But let's get back to our football coach for a moment. Because even more important than the relaxing and stimulating effects of the bath on the newborn is the potential this particular interaction seems to offer for cementing the paternal-infant bond.

The neglected—and neglectful—father.

However small their number, studies dealing with the father show his impact—for better or worse—to have been sorely underestimated. His sole purpose, they make clear, is not simply to work and earn—to pay the rent, the doctor bills, and ultimately, the college tuition fees. There is convincing evidence that the father's inadequacy or absence can erode the child's emotional well-being and that his wholesome, committed presence can help promote the mental health of his children.[7]

The syndrome of the "workaholic" father, who is physically present but emotionally unavailable during his children's formative years, appears to have reached crisis proportions in America. Assorted explanations are offered for this trend, which is cited in numerous commentaries on the decline of the nuclear family. The essential fact is that large numbers of men who are successful and highly competitive in professional life "tune out" when they reach their own front steps and are conveniently elsewhere when the time comes to check homework, play stickball, or attend the annual class play. In one study of white-collar workers and their one-year-old babies, the average time spent in meaningful interaction was reported to be *less than one minute per day!*

Are fathers innately less capable of loving and attaching to their children than mothers? It doesn't appear so. Although the pregnant woman has the advantage of nine months of intimate contact with the developing fetus and the stimulus of hormonal changes favoring bonding, current evidence suggests that given the opportunity to hold, cuddle, rock, and talk to their infants shortly after birth, new fathers will exhibit behavior just as tender and nurturant as that of their wives. (In fact, in some of the studies fathers tended to hold and rock their babies more than mothers did.)

"Given the opportunity . . ." Therein lies the catch. For, until very recently, few fathers were offered such opportunities; where they are, even now, cultural conditioning of males to be tough and emotionless may preclude their taking advantage of them.

The prospective father enters the relationship with several strikes against him. For the duration of pregnancy, he is an outsider; everything he knows about the fetus is learned secondhand. There is no swelling belly, no thrill of quickening, no twinge of Braxton-Hicks contractions to tell him that someone is already in there, waiting to be loved. In *Oneness and Separateness*, Louise J. Kaplan notes that fathers are "estranged from the emotions and fantasies that are so much a part of the pregnancy experience for a woman."[8]

In addition to feeling estranged from his baby, the prospective father may suspect that he has become a stranger to his wife, as well. Preoccupied with the unfamiliar stirrings of her body and the sudden urge to prepare a nest, the expectant woman finds that she has less and less time for the kind of communication upon which the strength of the marriage previously rested. Faced with a marital partner who not only looks considerably different but also appears to think and behave quite unlike her former self, the father-to-be may develop a silent resentment of the pregnancy and all it portends: the intrusion of another member into the close-knit family group, invasion of privacy, financial drain, and, above all, the beginnings of adult responsibility.

Unfortunately, things do not tend to get better following conventional hospital delivery. Says Kaplan: "After the birth of the baby, men are often deprived of the emotionally resonating experiences that would establish the bond between themselves and the newborn. It is not unusual for fathers to feel alienated from mother and baby for several months—sometimes for years." [9]

Angered at having to compete for his wife's attention (yet ashamed to admit himself capable of "childish" needs of his own), frustrated by her complete preoccupation with this being to whom he has not yet become truly attached, feeling clumsy and out of place in the nursery environment, the new father is almost inevitably drawn to seek out a setting where his talents will once again be acknowledged.

That he chooses the office as "his" place should come as a surprise to no one. Yet only a little forethought and awareness of cause-and-effect can yield lasting benefits. "Fathers whose feelings have been respected at the time of delivery, those who have been included in the process as important people," Lee Salk writes, "tend to be much more involved in the care of their children than the fathers who have been excluded. . . ." [10]

It is clear by now that husband participation—in childbirth education class and in the delivery room as labor coach—reduces the laboring woman's need for medication and heightens the emotional intensity of the birth. In the same way, development of essential caretaking skills by both partners during the postpartum period establishes a pattern of teamwork that allows the baby to bind them together as a couple, rather than tearing them apart. And the bath, by giving the new father a specific function to perform and an opportunity for close contact with the newborn during that crucial first hour when alertness reaches its peak, becomes a "resonating experience" that helps him (1) accept the baby as his and (2) begin to view the well-being of this third member of the triad as an extension of his own.

EARLY ESTABLISHMENT OF NURSING

After the bath, when both baby and mother are relaxed and revitalized, is the ideal time for nursing to begin. Studies of early extended contact are unanimous in their conclusion that mothers who are given their babies to suckle during the first hour after birth are more likely to continue nursing successfully during the months that follow. In view of the assortment of physiologic processes that affect, and are affected by, maternal-infant interaction during the so-called sensitive period, early establishment of suckling undoubtedly served to provide a built-in safeguard against later disturbances that might threaten the success of the nursing relationship . . . and newborn survival itself.

One thing is certain: The nursing mother in the present hospital setting needs all the help she can get!

Barriers to successful breast feeding. The frequency of failure of breast feeding in our culture contrasts sharply with its nearly universal success in less-developed areas where it is routine for mother and child to remain together throughout early infancy, nursing is on demand, and cultural traditions strongly support the nursing couple. In these societies, early suckling contact is *less* important, as in the absence of barriers a synchronous relationship will be built up anyway. Sadly, no such assurance exists for the modern, urbanized mother and child.

We have already examined some of the hospital routines that work against the effective establishment of nursing. To review, these include: overmedication of mothers and unnecessarily traumatic surgical interventions; postpartum separation of the infant from his parents; supplementary bottles in the hospital nursery; enforced feeding schedules; and general lack of support for the breast-feeding mother, resulting in an expectation of inadequacy which often proves self-fulfilling.

Although the rooting reflex and urge to suck are inborn, it takes some time and experience for both members of the nursing partnership to learn to coordinate their rhythms to ensure adequate intake. How a mother holds her infant affects his ability to grasp the areolar area, which determines the effectiveness of suckling and the amount of intake. The number of feedings and the duration of each will, in turn, affect prolactin secretion and influence the extent of the mother's milk production. Since some trial and error is required before the synchrony is perfected, it makes sense that this take place as early as possible, when the infant is at his hungriest, the mother's breasts are not yet painfully engorged, or overfull of milk, and there has been no opportunity for bad habits to develop.

The bad habit of most significance to the success or failure of breast feeding is, of course, a fondness for the artificial nipple. Bottle feeding involves a much less strenuous form of sucking than nursing at the breast; as a result, the bottle-fed infant receives large quantities of milk with relatively little effort on his part. It is interesting that, while exposure to the more generous flow of an artificial nipple before nursing has been established almost guarantees that the baby will lack interest in the breast, *this does not hold true* when bottle feeding is delayed.

The nursing mother can get her infant accustomed to an occasional supplemental bottle of formula later in the postpartum period without fear that he will establish a preference for it. By that time, the infant has learned to associate feeding with the smell and touch of his mother. Unless she decides to stop nursing and makes a clear effort to do so, he will continue to prefer the warmth and velvety texture of her breast to any other source of nourishment.

The newborn's active suckling during the first postpartum hour has been demonstrated time and again in nonviolent births. Whereas expectant mothers are traditionally warned that their babies will not be interested in nursing until about the third day of life, this need not be the case—as the following excerpt from an interview with a gentle birth mother shows: "He nursed for twenty minutes in the birthing room and then again during the first hour and a half we were together . . . he was very hungry and seemed to know how to suck. I noticed this especially because my first baby hadn't even learned how to suck until he was nearly twenty-four hours old, and it took the second at least half a day. Neither seemed hungry right after birth. . . ."

The nursing relationship. "If we read the biological program correctly," says Selma Fraiberg, "the period of breast feeding insured continuity of mothering as part of the program for the formation of human bonds."[11] In the hunter-gatherer societies of a million years ago—as in their present-day counterparts—babies remained in close skin contact with their mothers, were fed on demand, and had the opportunity to observe the world and be pleasantly jogged about during the woman's everyday foraging expeditions.

The relatively low protein content of breast milk meant that the newborn (especially during the first weeks of life) would be in nearly constant need of refueling; this, and the effectiveness of the hunger cry in eliciting a response, was his guarantee of frequent and satisfying interactions with his mother. Her ability to fulfill his needs in turn intensified her protective feelings and strengthened the bond between them.

Seen in the light of evolutionary adaptation, the limiting of newborn babies to feedings at strict four-hour (or even three-hour) intervals is clearly illogical. Infants need the physical contact and social exchange involved in breast or bottle feeding as much as they need the nourishment.

It is generally accepted that the more experienced a mother is, the more disinclined she will be to rely on schedules and the more likely to pick up and feed her baby whenever he *acts* hungry, regardless of what the clock says. Nursing mothers have an additional, strong impetus to interact frequently with their newborns because the babies get hungry faster than their formula-fed counterparts and demand their mothers' attention by crying at shorter intervals.*

Although the bottle-feeding mother has equivalent opportunities to hug and rock her infant while feeding, she is somewhat less likely than the nursing mother to spend time on these activities and more inclined to worry instead about the amount of milk consumed at each session and whether the baby brings up gas afterward. Breast-fed babies are able to derive considerable nutritional value out of even very short feedings and spend a good deal of time suckling just for the sheer joy of it. Since it is nearly impossible to overfeed a child on human milk alone—regardless of the duration of the feeding—it is thought that these infants

* While the higher protein content of cow's milk and bottled infant formulas allows for wider spacing of feedings (undeniably convenient for the busy mother), even the closest approximation of human milk is not nearly as satisfactory for meeting the real nutritional needs of infants, as will be shown in the next section.

may encounter fewer problems with obesity as they mature than infants fed artificial formulas.

In addition to being economical and convenient (nothing to mix, no heavy bottles to tote from place to place), as well as an aid to recovery and a pleasant sensual experience, nursing offers new mothers a welcome retreat from the rush of activities and community involvements that tend to compete with the baby for their attention.

Hunter-gatherer women, whose primary activity consisted of foraging for food, could discharge their responsibility to the community and nurture their infants at the same time. The contemporary woman whose day revolves around husband, job, older children, car pooling, and so forth, may find "making space" for the new baby a harder task than she had imagined. Regardless of the pace of her schedule, however, the breast-feeding mother knows that her infant is receiving several hours each day of loving, undivided attention.

Medical advantages. While the psychological benefits of nursing in terms of exchange of gaze, touching, and other attachment behaviors can, with sufficient determination on the mother's part, be duplicated in a bottle-feeding situation, its medical benefits cannot. Enough evidence is in at this point to allow us to state with certainty that *human milk is physiologically better for newborn babies* than any substitute science has come up with thus far. Lawrence M. Gartner, M.D., director of the neonatology division of New York's Albert Einstein College of Medicine, points out that: "Adaptation of milk secretion has taken place over millions of years of evolutionary experimentation to promote the survival of each mammalian species. It should come as no surprise to anyone that human milk—while completely inappropriate for meeting the nutritional needs of calves—is better able to support the survival of the human species than is cow's milk."

Studies dating back to the 1930s and 1940s showed reduced infant mortality and significantly reduced incidence of serious infections and hospitalizations among breast-fed babies. In one more recent study—which was controlled for social class to offset the argument that breast feeding in the United States is more common among better-educated, higher-income populations where newborn infection rates tend to be low anyway—infants who nursed had only half the incidence of ear infections, a fifteen-fold reduced rate of lower respiratory illnesses including croup, bronchitis, asthma, and pneumonia, and a notably lower incidence of gastrointestinal disease than the control group of formula-fed infants. Other studies have suggested that nursing significantly reduces the likelihood of that most feared of all baby-killers—sudden infant death syndrome (SIDS).

Prevention of infection in breast-fed babies results from (1) the relative cleanliness of breast milk and (2) the presence of certain specific components, not found in cow's milk, which work to retard the colonization of disease-causing bacteria and viruses. Among these are:

- The so-called *bifidus* factor, which promotes intestinal growth of a benign organism, *Lactobacillus bifidus,* preventing colonization by dangerous strains of bacteria
- An antistaphylococcal factor
- An enzyme that helps to kill streptococci
- Immunoglobulins with antibody activity against specific human pathogens

The human milk concentration of immunoglobulins is highest in colostrum, then gradually declines as nursing progresses and the infant builds up his own store of antibodies. Continuation of nursing is assured by a fascinating chain of events; if, for example, the mother eats food contaminated with a new strain of bacteria or virus, her immune mechanisms immediately respond by manufacturing antibodies for its inactivation. The antibodies are excreted in her milk, while contact during frequent feedings ensures that both mother and infant are protected from infection.

No allergy to human milk protein has ever been documented. By contrast, cow's milk allergy is thought to develop in as many as one in every ten bottle-fed infants and children. Furthermore, allergic children have been found to be at greater risk of developing related infections than the average youngster.

Even the basic nutritional components of human and cow's milk are known to be substantially different, with the latter higher in protein (calves grow much more quickly than human babies) and mineral content (the greater salt concentration places a strain on infant kidneys, particularly if the baby is premature) and significantly lower in iron, certain vitamins, and amino acids. There are also considerable differences in digestibility, due to the large amounts of curd formed when babies are fed whole cow's milk.*

Summing up: breast versus bottle. In view of the emotional and physiologic advantages spelled out on the previous pages, the casual reader might be led to suspect that we believe breast feeding is for everyone . . . we do not. There are instances—admittedly few —in which nursing is medically inadvisable. (These include the presence of certain serious metabolic disorders, such as phenylketonuria, in the infant, a history of breast surgery in the mother, active viral infection requiring separation of the mother-infant pair, and so forth.) Far more common than the medical contraindications, and equally valid, are personal objections to breast feeding based on such considerations as the demands imposed by an inflexible nine-to-five job or negative feedback from the woman's husband and family.

Nursing should be a joy—not a chore. There is no question that a baby stands to gain more from a mother who interacts warmly and comfortably with him while bottle feeding than if the same woman were to grit her teeth and nurse him because the textbooks all say she should. Furthermore, manufacturers of infant formulas are constantly readjusting their components to conform more closely to human milk, with the result that today's formulas are far more digestible and less likely to provoke an allergic response than those our mothers used.

What we *are* saying is simply this: Do give serious thought to the idea of breast feeding your baby. And if you decide you want to try, then begin early. Gentle childbirth mothers who initiate nursing within the first hour after birth encounter few problems with it; mothers who wait until the following day—or until the next "scheduled" hospital feeding time—may find that conditions then are far less favorable.

EXTENDED POSTPARTUM CONTACT

Why is the nursing staff generally so eager to take the newborn away from its parents and place it in a plastic box in the nursery? Because we, the pediatricians, have been successful in inculcating the concept that

---

* The difference is narrowed when preheated formulas are used.

infants must be under close medical observation for six or more hours after birth, regardless of their condition. Now that we ourselves know better, we wonder why the policy is so inflexible. . . .

Marshall H. Klaus, M.D.

A child is born, examined, and pronounced healthy. And then —what? In a family-centered environment, the baby remains close to her parents during the recovery period and rooms in at her mother's discretion for the remainder of the hospital stay. During this period, mother and infant begin to develop the synchrony required for effective establishment of nursing; both parents gain confidence in their caretaking skills; and, if hospital rules are sufficiently flexible, the baby can be introduced to her apprehensive older brothers and sisters as well.*

Contact during the recovery period, like that immediately following birth, has special importance in obliterating the fantasies of pregnancy and the stress of labor, and establishing the baby as a person of significance in her parents' eyes. The couple have, after all, just spent over nine months anticipating the arrival, guessing at the sex, and wondering about the appearance of this particular infant. After the elation of birth, there is a tremendous letdown when the baby is taken from her mother's arms and handed over to the nursery personnel for "observation." The wife of a pediatrician remembers: "My older daughter was born by natural childbirth, and it was a beautiful experience. But immediately after she left my body she was whisked away and placed in an incubator. Since my husband was a physician, he was allowed to go along . . . but of course I was unable to. I can recall yelling,

---

* Child-care authorities are overwhelmingly in favor of sibling visitation as a way of lessening the trauma of separation for older children and their mothers. Youngsters who have been poorly prepared (or who feel left out and abandoned by their mother's departure, *however* carefully explained) will naturally look upon the new baby as a stranger and rival for their parents' affection. Children under three years of age in particular often have real fears that their mother has been taken away by force, will be harmed, even that they will never see her again. On the mother's part, concern about the effect of the separation on the rest of her family may interfere with her enjoyment of the newborn, retard establishment of nursing, and impel her to return home before she is physically ready to resume her old role.

When siblings are allowed daily postpartum visits and made to feel a part of the birth, the process of adjustment goes much more smoothly for the entire family. Not only is there a restoration of confidence in the mother's well-being and her continuing love, but the early involvement of older children in the care of the youngest encourages growth of attachment between the offspring paralleling the growth of the stronger parental-infant bond.

'Is everything all right? Whom does she look like?' To this day, I haven't stopped feeling resentful about it. . . ."

Extended contact on succeeding days provides what may be the first-time mother's only chance to refine her techniques of feeding, diapering, and dressing the newborn in a relaxed setting, with the help of maternity staff. In De Chateau's study, those primiparous mothers who had roomed in with their babies judged themselves, one day prior to discharge, as being more competent in baby care—and, consequently, less dependent upon outside assistance—than control mothers whose infants had remained in the nursery. The rooming-in mothers were also more inclined to breast feed their babies and felt themselves better able to interpret their infants' cries.

Other studies have demonstrated that infants who room in cry less often than those left in the nursery (a result, it is thought, of quicker intervention by the caregiver and the willingness of mothers to feed on demand) and accustom themselves more readily to the caregiver's day-night rhythm. In one report, there was a significant increase in breast feeding and reduction in the number of anxious telephone calls to the pediatrician or nurse-practitioner in the early weeks following hospital acceptance of a rooming-in (sometimes known as "permissive nursery") arrangement.

When the father is encouraged to share in these activities, the effects, like those of the bath, are probably permanent. Lee Salk writes: "Hospitals ought to give a class, specifically for fathers, on how to feed, bathe, and diaper the baby. If these skills are taught only to the mothers and if they are then expected to teach the fathers, the relationships are altered, and not for the better. Many problems with sex-role stereotyping in child care and rearing could be avoided by bringing in the fathers from the start." [12]

The sense of involvement produced by repeated handling of the newborn in the early postpartum period does not cease when the baby is brought home. Gentle birth fathers, say the investigators, are more willing to shoulder the mundane, even distinctly unappealing tasks involved in caring for a new baby, as well as the "fun" things that fathers have always done, because *they already view themselves as effective parents.*

Since, as we have observed, competence breeds concern (just as the lack of it invites indifference), there is every reason to expect that the father who spoons cereal with expertise and does not flinch from an occasional messy diaper will, in later years, also find time to coach Little League, sign report cards, and attend PTA meetings and ballet recitals.

"BUT IS IT BETTER?"

"Well," said the pediatrician I was interviewing, "you've proved that gentle delivery is not harmful to babies. And, O.K., the parents like it well enough. But can you prove it's *better* than what we already have?"

Is nonviolent birth medically superior to the standard obstetrical model? Without more hard data, the only possible answer at the present time is: We don't know. Despite certain advantages such as the "bacterial interference" created by direct skin contact and lack of trauma associated with clearing of nasopharyngeal mucus, we cannot say for certain that gentle childbirth is statistically safer than its alternative, *if* the alternative is one in which interventions are minimized, little medication is used, and there is continuous, close observation by the physician or midwife in charge. (That most conventional births do not meet these qualifications goes without saying.)

But each of us is more than just a mechanized bundle of nerves and tissues. The emotional and behavioral components cannot be completely separated from the physiologic; they remain intertwined throughout the long passage from cradle—or infant warmer—to grave.

Is gentle birth better for babies?

Let's take a closer look.

NOTES

1. Marshall H. Klaus and John H. Kennell, *Maternal-Infant Bonding* (St. Louis: C. V. Mosby, 1976), p. 48.
2. Michael J. Hughey, Thomas W. McElin, and Todd Young, "Maternal and Fetal Outcome of Lamaze-prepared Patients," *Obstetrics and Gynecology*, June 1978, p. 646.
3. Ruth Wilf, "Fulfilling the Needs of Families in a Hospital Setting: Can It Be Done?" in Lee Stewart and David Stewart, eds., *21st Century Obstetrics Now!* (Chapel Hill, N.C.: NAPSAC, Inc., 1977), p. 51.

4. Leboyer, *Birth Without Violence,* p. 51.

5. Ibid., p. 50.

6. Penelope Leach, *Your Baby and Child: From Birth to Age Five* (New York: Alfred A. Knopf, 1978), p. 29.

7. Julius Segal and Herbert Yahraes, *A Child's Journey: Forces That Shape the Lives of Our Young* (New York: McGraw-Hill, 1978), pp. 106–107.

8. Louise J. Kaplan, *Oneness and Separateness: From Infant to Individual* (New York: Simon & Schuster, 1978), p. 66.

9. Ibid., p. 68.

10. Lee Salk, "The Need for Humanized Perinatal Care," *Contemporary Ob/Gyn,* April 1977, pp. 110–14.

11. Selma Fraiberg, *Every Child's Birthright: In Defense of Mothering* (New York: Basic Books, 1977), p. 28.

12. Salk, "The Need for Humanized Perinatal Care," pp. 110–14.

Courtesy of Pat Levy,
Lamaze-Leboyer Childbirth Education Center

8 · About the Babies

These children born in silence and love—what becomes of them?

Frederick Leboyer, Birth Without Violence

Visit a typical exercise class for expectant and new mothers at the Lamaze-Leboyer Childbirth Education Center in Mount Kisco, New York. In the sunny, airy room—much like a ballet studio, except for the prevalence of parenting books and baby carriers —ten or twelve women will be doing stretching and breathing exercises with their instructor, Pat Levy, ASPO/ICEA. Off to one side, cozily settled in infant seats or on comforters spread across the carpeted floor, are some five or six babies ranging in age from three weeks on up. Some are dozing, hands clutched around rattles or fuzzy toys. Others are watching the exercising women with bright, alert eyes. A few, cuddled in slings against their mothers' chests or backs, may actually be participating in the simpler routines. What is unique about this scene?

Not one of the babies is crying.

THE ROLE OF TEMPERAMENT

Differences in temperament among newborn babies, and the factors contributing to them, began to receive real scientific attention with the studies of psychiatrists Alexander Thomas and Stella Chess in the 1950s. After following a large number of middle- and working-class children from early infancy into adolescence, these investigators concluded that wide variations in temperament ("easy," "difficult," "slow to warm up") were clearly evident in babies as early as two or three months of age, and that these differences—which tended to remain consistent as the child matured—had a profound effect on parental behavior and quality of caregiving.

Prior to this point, alongside the belief that infants were passive lumps of clay to be shaped by their parents and other environmental forces, was a general assumption that regular patterns of behavior were "normal" for newborns. With just a little coaxing, it was felt, almost any baby could be made to fall into a comfortable rhythm of sleeping, waking, and feeding, punctuated by brief bursts of crying when his immediate wants were not met.

(And some excuses for crying were felt to be more acceptable than others. Being wet, cold, or in pain from a loose diaper pin constituted sufficient grounds for demanding an adult's intervention; simple want of human company did not.)

Naturally, the mother of an infant who cried incessantly, slept in short spurts, and appeared hungry only an hour or two after feedings could only conclude that she had failed in some terrible way. To make matters worse, a great many babies who are easily upset are also difficult to soothe, so that the parents receive little confirmation of their effectiveness, regardless of the amount of time spent cuddling, rocking, or walking the agitated baby.

Observing that their nervous efforts to calm him simply prolonged the misery, a couple with no previous children and few opportunities to watch other parents' difficult babies in action might well become convinced that theirs was abnormal (hyperactivity is the most frequently heard excuse) and carry that conviction over into their parenting.*

Luckily, (1) the idea that newborns exhibit a wide range of "normal" behaviors is beginning to gain acceptance; (2) even ultrasensitive babies generally outgrow their miserable phase by the end of the fourth month; and (3) favorable environmental conditions can assist parents in overcoming their ambivalent feelings, preventing a mixture of concern, anger, and guilt from progressing to actual withdrawal of attachment.

When factors such as a stable marital relationship, financial security, and group support permit a couple to hang on to their patience and good humor long enough to restructure their expectations, they can often adjust their caregiving patterns to conform to the infant's needs for stimulation. They may even, as T. Berry Brazelton has so nicely pointed out, be able to *teach* the sensitive newborn to suck his thumb, find consolation in a fuzzy blanket, or seek out other means of calming himself.

When, on the other hand, a "fussy" baby's home life is colored by poverty, brutality, and/or emotional stress, his chances for emotional—and at times even physical—survival are substantially lessened. The concept that an infant's temperament can have a sizable impact on the responses of his caregivers is backed by devastating evidence from the histories of children who were beaten, starved, or even allowed to die of neglect.

Child abuse is a disease of society most often attributed to the failure of parents to cope with the normal demands imposed by their young. However, recent reports suggest that certain babies' demands may exceed the normal limit, and that rejection in these cases is more of a two-way street.

Richard Q. Bell of the National Institute of Mental Health notes that "it is quite typical to find that other children in the family of an abused child are not abused." While "the stimulus characteristics of the child do not operate by themselves to induce mistreatment," emphasizes Bell, these characteristics may play a role

---

* It is noteworthy that the opposite extreme—the baby who lies in his crib staring straight ahead or sleeps for prolonged periods and interacts with his parents only briefly—also has an off-putting effect on new mothers and fathers. In their discussion of prematurity, Klaus and Kennell mention the need to caution the parents of premature infants not to feel rejected if the baby refuses to be aroused by their attempts at establishing contact. This will come in time.

comparable to that of parental instability or a brutish environment: "Constant fussing, strange and highly irritating crying, or other exasperating behaviors, were often reported for the one child subject to abuse in the family. Some children were abused in successive foster homes in which they were placed after the initial abuse. No other child had been abused previously in these foster homes."[1]

Sources of irritability. What makes certain babies less regular in their patterns and more inclined to grumpiness than others? We have already touched upon some of the factors:

Infants who room in with their mothers cry less and are more easily comforted than newborns who spend most of their hospital stay in the nursery. These babies develop confidence in the quick response of the caretaker and believe that their basic needs will be met without excessive fussing on their part. (Similarly, mothers given extra postpartum contact with their infants learn to distinguish the signals for food, contact comfort, and so forth, are better able to judge how much stimulation the baby requires, and gradually discover which techniques of quieting are most likely to be effective.)

In addition, several studies have shown that babies of mothers who have received substantial dosages of medication for delivery are more easily startled, cry more readily, and take longer to calm down afterward than babies of less medicated mothers. Infants who have experienced unusually long and physically traumatic labors are likewise inclined to be irritable, as well as to sleep for shorter periods and encounter problems with nursing or bottle feeding. Since in many instances a long labor, increased medication, and poor feeding all go together, it is extremely difficult to separate cause from effect and distinguish the primary basis for newborn irritability.

Complicating the picture still further is the question of the mother's emotional state before, during, and after parturition. There is some basis for believing that anxious mothers tend to have anxious babies, and often longer and/or more difficult labors, as well. Lee Salk and Rita Kramer note that "The idea of the nine months preceding birth as a time in which development proceeds only along predetermined lines, unaffected by the life around it, no longer fits the evidence. Not only is the fetus influenced by the mother's nutritional state, and not only can it be affected by certain viral infections and drugs, but an impressive number of studies show that a mother's state of mind, through related physiological manifestations—such as the hormonal changes that are associated with severe anxiety—can affect the fetus too."[2]

What all of this breaks down to is that each and every infant is born with a unique behavioral style, as individual as the features on his face. Like other constitutional traits, temperament is partly determined by the genes the child has inherited . . . but only partly. The rest is a reflection of his mother's condition—emotional as well as physiologic—during pregnancy, any drugs or diseases transmitted to the fetus, trauma experienced in the birth canal, and (the most easily modified feature and the one we are stressing here) the quality of his first encounters with extrauterine life.

What the newborn brings to the relationship with his parents is then modified by their responses to *him:* how they perceive his outgoingness or reserve, what conclusions they draw from his range of cries. And, coloring all the rest, the degree of sensitivity and flexibility they are able to bring to their parenting.

PERSISTENCE OF PATTERNS

"An emotional, volatile young lady," grinned the pediatrician as he watched my daughter, then aged roughly two months, respond with more than the usual degree of outrage to her first DPT immunization. "You're in for quite a time with her," he added, "but at least [softening the blow somewhat] it won't be dull!"

And, of course, he was right. Living with Amy has been neither easy nor dull, because the results of the developmental studies only confirm what mothers have suspected for centuries: Although the design becomes increasingly intricate and details may shift, the basic outlines of a child's temperament remain comparatively stable from babyhood onward.

This in no way implies that a placid baby will necessarily become a passive adult, or that the infant who responds to every noise with a startle will be unable to sit still in school. What it does mean is that the raw materials of personality, far from being entirely blank, already have shape and texture, color and consistency, in the first months of life.

What happens to that raw material, the extent to which each child is able to realize the full range of his possibilities, is very much dependent upon parental influence (and, in later years, upon the influence of teachers and the child's peers). With sympathy and encouragement, the withdrawn baby may become an energetic participant in group play. With patience and understanding, the driving, extremely active infant can be shown ways of channeling his enormous energies into creative and socially acceptable outlets. As L. Alan Sroufe, professor of child psychology at the University of Minnesota's Institute of Child Development, points out, "A child who has a rapid tempo may be seething with anger, hostile to other children, unable to control his or her impulses, and filled with feelings of worthlessness. But a child who has a rapid tempo also may be eager, spirited, effective, and a pleasure to others, and may like him- or herself." [3]

Many so-called miracles in the treatment of brain-injured children have been achieved after the dogged refusal of one or both parents to listen to the wisdom of specialists and the counsel of friends to "give up . . . he'll never walk, talk, tie his shoes, learn the alphabet," and so forth. Because these parents did not give up but continued to work with the child, the youngsters frequently proved able to master the simple tasks of caring for themselves which—while not everybody's equivalent of a college diploma— were *their* passport to a life with dignity and freedom from institutionalization.

That parental direction and support can have a similarly powerful effect on the emotional and intellectual development of normal, healthy babies and children should be self-evident. One would be hard-pressed to find a study that did not point to the importance of early verbal communication for acquisition of language, opportunities to manipulate toys and other objects for developing a sense of mastery over the environment, and frequent hugging and other demonstrations of affection in establishing the capacity for adult love.

Sroufe, author of *Knowing and Enjoying Your Baby,* underlines the view shared by other investigators that, whether "highly active or placid, cuddly or stiff," the baby who is doing well is the one whose secure attachment to and trust in his caregiver promotes exploration of the environment and eventual belief in his own competence. Studies by his Minnesota team showed a dramatic relationship between the quality of a baby's attachment at eighteen months of age and his adaptive functioning as a two-year-old: "Children who were assessed as secure in their attachment as infants were much more enthusiastic and persistent and showed more positive feelings than did children who had earlier been assessed as anxiously attached. The children who had been securely attached showed fewer negative emotions, and in a situation where assistance was essential, they were more compliant, threw fewer tantrums, and ignored or opposed their mothers less often. In contrast to the anxiously attached groups, they showed no aggression."[4]

Furthermore, according to Sroufe, the child who is functioning well at one age level is likely to function equally well at the next, regardless of the behavioral component being evaluated. Toddlers are essentially more highly developed versions of the persons they were in infancy; four-year-olds are very much the same individuals they were as toddlers. The self-esteem that results from sensitive caregiving in infancy and toddlerhood appears to enable a child to tolerate stress better and recover more quickly from crisis situations. "Even when floundering," the psychologist adds, "some children may not lose their sense that they can affect the environment and that, ultimately, they will be all right."[5]

The last comment is particularly interesting in view of the frequently heard warning that nonviolent childbirth will create a generation of young adults so "soft" that they will lack the stamina to battle for a seat on the subway. Life is full of conflict, the argument goes, and children must be taught to face it from the start.

Replies pediatrician John H. Kennell: "There is a tremendous tendency in this country to apply to very young children what you expect at 21 years of age. So independence is a very highly valued trait. But all newborns want and need to cling to their mothers. . . . And the babies who are allowed to do it, those who are held and closely attended to at the beginning of the first year of life, are the same children who will be able to separate from their mothers more easily when the time comes. They—and not the kids who are thrust from the nest before they are ready—will ultimately be the successful ones."

GENTLE BIRTH AND THE DEVELOPMENT OF COMPETENCE

When you're very little, if you have a sense that you're utterly lovable, then you can face the world.

Marshall H. Klaus, M.D.

How have gentle birth babies performed on standardized development tests? Do the responses of the parents remain consistent when subjected to more thorough analysis?

Although no data are currently available from American institutions, there is one study from France that may prove predictive of future investigations. This survey of 120 of Leboyer's original group of babies and their mothers was conducted by psychologist Danielle Rapoport under the auspices of the French National Center for Scientific Research, using an adaptation of Arnold Gesell's development inventory.

The children, chosen at random from one thousand patient records, were aged one, two, and three years at the time of testing. All had been delivered at the same government-supported clinic to mothers who had no prior knowledge of nonviolent birth techniques and no reason to request such innovations for themselves. Sixty-five percent of the women had never even met Leboyer before going into labor; their hospitalizations had merely coincided with his being on call. Testing was in the form of standardized psychomotor examinations, observations of each child's play behavior in various situations, and a parent questionnaire and interview. Roughly summarized, the results were as follows:

On a scale of 129, the mean development quotient (DQ) of the children was 106, somewhat higher than the general average of 100. Average walking age was thirteen months, as compared to an average of fourteen or fifteen months in the population at large. Sensorimotor coordination was uniformly excellent. A surprising and unexplained finding was the pronounced ambidexterity of a great many of the three-year-olds, which facilitated their manipulation of toys and other objects.

While toilet training and self-feeding were advanced, the speech of the children tested showed the normal range of variations. Only four mothers reported problems with feeding or sleep disturbances, and there was a notable absence of reports of colic or irritable crying during the newborn period.

The couples' attitudes displayed freedom from the kind of anxieties about parenting that psychologists have increasingly come to regard as normal. This *despite the fact that, for 64 percent of the mothers, this was the first baby.* Ninety-five percent of the parents commented on their good luck and/or the lack of serious problems, emphasizing instead the child's calm and cheerful disposition, cooperativeness, ability to feed and dress himself, and other positive traits. The research team received only two requests for consultations outside the survey—both in reference to other siblings!

In addition to mentioning their easy relationship with the child, parents expressed gratefulness for the quality of the birth experience itself.* All but six of the women (three of whom had been anesthetized and were unable to respond fully to the survey) freely described the event as extraordinary, affecting, or profound. Each reported that she hoped to give birth to any future children by the same method and would recommend it for other women, as well. Particular mention was made of the pleasure of having the baby in direct skin contact on the mother's abdomen immediately after birth and of the more relaxed pacing of usual postpartum routines.

Fathers, too, appeared to take an exceptional interest in the children. Eighty percent accompanied their partners to the interviews, even though the presence of the father had not been specifically requested. (And this, remember, was not a particularly family-centered environment, but an ordinary French hospital in which father participation was not generally encouraged.)

Regarding the diversity of the babies themselves, Rapoport notes that "at no point in the study did I have the impression of being confronted with a sort of 'Leboyer baby' typology." Far from being uniformly passive, "Each child in this group was as different from the others as are children in the general population. The calm of the first few weeks rapidly gives way in response to the variety of environments and parental personalities, to the

---

* Rapoport notes that the two are interrelated, that is, a woman's perception of a birth experience influences her subsequent perception of the child it produces.

variety of modes of adaptation and infant personalities. Being born without violence seems to have provided these children with conditions particularly favorable to their development."[6]

Does gentle birth provide a sound base for early psychomotor development? Can it, by inviting both responsiveness in the baby and sensitivity in the caretaker, encourage the development of competence? From the study just described, it certainly would appear so. Let's hear what some other parents have to say.

The parents speak. "Every couple of weeks, another physician will come up to me and ask, 'Do you really think all this extra care matters in the long run?' And," notes Grover, "my response is always the same. 'Ask the parents.'"

I did. Here, from among the many—similar—replies I received, is a typical sampling:

". . . Andrew's birth was so calm and relaxed. The experience was a delight. We are all closer because of it."

"Our first baby was very difficult—colicky and generally crabby. We feel we owe part of the difference to our maturity and advance knowledge, but the Leboyer delivery definitely set the mood. . . ."

". . . my husband was so excited about the baby that he kept her up late into the night, watching movies on TV with him!"

"Ellen was very calm and relaxed from the first moment. Nursed well, and seemed to enjoy our company. . . ."

". . . a very easy baby. Anything you did or anywhere you decided to take her was fine with her."

"My obstetrician remarked afterward that ours was among the first gentle births that he had participated in. He was very impressed by the baby's responsiveness and kept telling us how lucky we were."

"The contrast between our first child and this baby was apparent in the eyes. Helena's eyes were bright and alert right from the start. . . ."

". . . my initial reaction to the Leboyer method was that it was enjoyable, especially for my husband. Recently, however, so many people have commented to me that Michael is an unusually good-natured and peaceful baby that I have begun to reflect more upon the impact of the gentle birth on him. Although I realize that many things—my easy pregnancy, short labor, uncomplicated delivery, and the baby's inner makeup—

must have contributed to the calm, our gentle handling of him after birth seemed to be an integral part of the whole process."

NOTES

1. Richard Q. Bell, "Contributions of Human Infants to Caregiving and Social Interaction," in Michael Lewis and Leonard A. Rosenblum, eds., *Origins of Behavior: The Effect of the Infant on Its Caregiver* (New York: Wiley), 1974.
2. Lee Salk and Rita Kramer, *How to Raise a Human Being* (New York: Random House, 1969), p. 50.
3. L. Alan Sroufe, "Attachment and the Roots of Competence," *Human Nature,* October 1978, p. 56.
4. Ibid.
5. Ibid.
6. Danielle Rapoport, "The Controversial Leboyer Method," *The Female Patient,* June 1978, p. 86.

Courtesy of Nancy Berezin

9 · Choosing a Sympathetic Practitioner

> *In the practical application of the Leboyer Method we find ourselves confronting material deficiencies, such as the lack of aware, qualified personnel and the resistance of physicians who are only just beginning to open up to the psychosomatic aspect of their art and the dimensions of the unconscious. In addition, we must deal with society's view of childhood, and the way its mores allow women to experience their bodies, their sexuality, and their maternity.*
>
> Danielle Rapoport

Our argument is ended. There is no more evidence to be cited in favor of nonviolence . . . the choice must come, as Leboyer says, from within.

In the event, however, that you have reached at least a tentative decision in favor of gentle birth in a family-centered setting, your next step will be to find a physician or midwife sincerely committed to these goals. The following chapter is designed not to provide a comprehensive profile of the ideal birth attendant—every couple's needs are different—but rather to point out a few of the pitfalls and offer a suggestion or two, based on the experiences of other expectant parents, on how to proceed.

The first one is:

"You catch more flies with honey than with vinegar."

The nurse-midwife, with her orientation toward healthy pregnancies and family care, may very well dim the lights for delivery, speak in hushed tones, and place the baby on the mother's abdomen as a matter of course. If these things are not part of her ordinary routine, she is at least likely to be open to suggestions. By contrast, the physician who has been trained to regard pregnancy as a disease—particularly if he is middle-aged or older and a board-certified obstetrician—may be considerably less amenable to such innovations.

Obstetrician Robert A. Bradley, a pioneer of the husband-wife team approach to childbirth and one of the first physicians in this country to speak out against the dangers of excessive obstetrical anesthesia and analgesia, recognized this characteristic inflexibility when he noted: "Most doctors are egocentric. This is nearly a necessity in the practice of medicine for psychological reasons. You wouldn't want a fumbling, uncertain Caspar Milquetoast in charge of your health or life. Most doctors in established practice bitterly resent lay people teaching them another way of doing obstetrics. You are insulting them by implying that what they are doing and have been doing for years is wrong and your way is right."[1]

Bradley's comments were addressed to couples seeking a prepared, unmedicated childbirth experience—at one time a rare commodity in the United States. Today, expectant parents in most cities have their choice of childbirth education teachers and obstetricians who advocate (or at least say they advocate) minimal anesthesia and analgesia, and husband participation. That such changes have come about in the twenty years since publication of Marjorie Karmel's enthusiastic *Thank you, Dr. Lamaze* is evidence not only of the success of consumer pressure in obstetrics but also of the willingness of individual physicians to risk change . . . once they have become convinced that the safety of their patients is not being jeopardized.

The physician who chooses to specialize in family-centered gentle childbirth will be the kind of person who can accept the patient and her husband as responsible adults, who are even more concerned than he that everything should go well.

For some practitioners, the changeover from the traditional, paternalistic doctor-patient relationship to one of mutual respect and cooperation has come naturally—almost as a relief. For others, it remains an impossibility. For the majority, those who already advocate childbirth education and the couple approach but are reluctant to make waves among their colleagues by trying a new technique of delivery, or who regard the additional minutes spent in the labor room and overseeing the massage and bath as a useless waste of their time, a campaign of friendly-but-stubborn persuasion works best.

The patient who arrives at her first prenatal visit with a list of demands a mile long and loudly threatens to go elsewhere if the doctor does not immediately agree to meet every one of them will probably be advised to do just that. On the other hand, the patient who proceeds tactfully—having judged that this is an individual with whom she can work, one who is already in agreement with her on the majority of issues and is willing to give her views a fair hearing*—stands a good chance of persuading her physician to try a nonviolent birth.

Starting from scratch. Suppose you have just moved from the city to the suburbs—a not uncommon situation for a young couple about to have their first baby. Your trusted obstetrician-gynecologist or family physician is a hundred miles away; how do you go about choosing a new one?

Well, you *could* look in the Yellow Pages of the telephone directory or ask the woman folding towels next to you at the Laundromat. But a much more reasonable method would be to call the local hospital and ask in the department of obstetrics and gynecology for a list of the physicians on staff who are currently performing Leboyer-type deliveries, or have a reputation for interest in prepared childbirth and family-centered care.

An alternate route would be to write to either the International Childbirth Education Association (ICEA) or the American Society

---

* If not, she certainly *should* look elsewhere without delay!

for Psychoprophylaxis in Obstetrics (ASPO).* Both organizations offer an assortment of helpful services, including lists of the childbirth options available at various county hospitals and the names of physicians in the locality who are most involved in this approach.

Assuming you trust her advice, asking a close friend for the name of her obstetrician might be another good way to begin. Before making the appointment, however, it's a wise idea to learn something more about his approach: Was he with your friend on a fairly regular basis during labor, or did he arrive only in time to "catch" the baby? What sort of anesthesia does he generally recommend, and *what was actually used* in her case? Is he affiliated with a medical center that has adequate support facilities, in case of emergency? Does he have an associate physician or midwife covering for him at all times? Was childbirth education emphasized? Was your friend's husband not only allowed but actually encouraged to participate in both labor and delivery? Were the lights lowered for birth, and was the nursing staff cooperative in allowing the new parents plenty of time to touch, caress, and admire the baby?

Once you are satisfied that the obstetrician seems to be the sort of individual you are seeking, go ahead and make the appointment. Plan, though, on a reasonably thorough discussion of the points just listed and any others that may particularly concern you at the time of the first prenatal visit. Try to select an hour when your husband can also be present.

Says Paul Spierling, M.D., chairman of the department of obstetrics and gynecology, Northern Westchester Hospital Center, New York: "At our first meeting, I ask the patient and her husband to go home and think about what will constitute a good obstetrical experience for them. When they've drawn up a preliminary list of what they want, we go over it point by point and I either say 'okay' or I explain why in my opinion something isn't a particularly good idea. Generally speaking, most of the requests relate to things I've always done . . . or have done for several years at least, simply because they're good obstetrics. I do, however, occasionally draw the line. My rule of thumb is: If you can give

* ICEA, P.O. Box 20852, Milwaukee, Wisconsin 53220
ASPO, 1411 K Street, N.W., Suite 200, Washington, DC 20005
Or call the branch office listed in your telephone directory.

the couple a *medically valid* reason for your decision, something that lends itself to clear explanation, then you're probably on the right track. If, however, all you can think of are vague generalities to support your choice of a procedure, then it's probably time to reconsider that procedure."

This is the age of the "second opinion." Physicians have grown accustomed to being intensively questioned by their patients; they expect that at times a personality clash or a simple difference of opinion will occur. If a problem in communication is self-evident and you decide that, contrary to expectation, the first physician you contact is not for you, rest assured: You will not be the first to switch! Often as not, the doctor himself will be glad to provide you with the name of a colleague whose ideas are more in keeping with your own.

Individual or group practice? This is a very personal decision. Some women cannot tolerate having several doctors, while others feel perfectly comfortable even in a very large practice where the chances of meeting all of the partners beforehand are slim. Ideally, of course, the couple should have the opportunity to get to know all of the group members well in advance of delivery. Since most obstetrical practices consist of no more than three or four physicians and/or midwives, simple rotation of prenatal appointments solves the problem *provided all partners agree on the conditions of delivery, the parents' role, medication, and similar points.*

Almost invariably, the physicians mentioned in this book as advocating gentle delivery operate with associates who also employ the techniques. Thus, the patient and her husband can be certain that their wishes will be honored even if the baby is born while their primary doctor is on vacation, off call, or attending a medical conference.

The alternative—taking a chance that the physician on call that night will be sympathetic to the couple's decision and knowledgeable about gentle birth procedures—is risky, as it would be with any departure from the obstetrical norm. It is far more likely that a physician with no experience in the method will insist on doing things his way, rather than take a chance with the patient of a colleague. Not only is this attitude justified on medical grounds (even the staunchest supporters of Leboyer believe that everyone on the obstetrical team should feel comfortable with the approach before going ahead), but a woman who is already in hard labor is really not emotionally up to an argument!

The family friend. Up to now we have concentrated upon the criteria used in selecting a new physician. But suppose you already have a doctor you know and like (the one who delivered your previous children, for example), and you don't want to switch. Yet you would like your next baby delivered gently. He disapproves.

Don't give up. You have nine months to plan for the birth of this child, and a lot can be accomplished in that space of time. Show your physician the evidence presented in this book; suggest he read Leboyer's *Birth Without Violence,* or see a filmed account of gentle birth in a family-centered setting. Explain that you are flexible enough in *your* thinking to accept a necessary change in plan, should the need arise. This may persuade him to unbend a little and give the matter more serious consideration.

Best of all, ask him to observe a nonviolent delivery for himself, speak to the physician or midwife in charge, and examine the baby. . . . The magic of gentle birth lies in its simplicity; a little open-mindedness is all that is required.

But that, of course, is the rarest commodity of all.

NOTE

1. Robert A. Bradley, *Husband-Coached Childbirth* (New York: Harper & Row, 1974), p. 195.

Afterword

> *It is now over seventy years since Freud discovered that the most severe and crippling emotional disorders of adult life have their genesis in early childhood. During the past thirty years our studies have led us deeper and deeper into the unknown territories of childhood, into infancy and early childhood and the origins of personality. We now know that those qualities that we call "human"—the capacity for enduring love and the exercise of conscience—are not given in human biology; they are the achievement of the earliest human partnership, that between a child and his parents.*
>
> Selma Fraiberg,
> Every Child's Birthright:
> In Defense of Mothering

Over and over again in *The Gentle Birth Book* we have stressed the need for flexibility in obstetrical practice, on the part of both the institutions in which babies are born and the individuals chosen by the parents to attend those births. Now the time has come to talk briefly about another kind of flexibility, one more directly involving the parents themselves.

As the Lamaze movement was only a short time ago, gentle birth is presently in its infancy. But it is steadily gaining strength . . . and strange things sometimes happen to reform movements as they mature. Above all, we feel it would be tragic if Leboyer's *techniques* were to become excessively ritualized and the underlying message overlooked, that message being that the baby is a person, too, with needs and, as Selma Fraiberg has pointed out, a "birthright" to her parents' love.

Whatever has been learned over the past decade in studies of newborn behavior and parental-infant attachment (and the amount has certainly been formidable) only leads us to the conclusion that much more remains to be understood. Bonding itself is clearly the result of a myriad of influences, not the least of which is the enormous and still-underrated influence of the newborn herself.

Impressions formed at birth, however deep and far-reaching their impact, do not remain permanently fixed but are forever being reinforced or altered by events later in the relationship.

In closing, therefore, it seems appropriate to address a word to those couples who—hampered by a reluctant obstetrician, a stubborn hospital administration, or an unexpected medical complication—may fail in their desire to obtain a nonviolent birth.

Although we firmly believe that gentle childbirth can provide an enriching experience for parents and babies, the human capacity for attachment is infinite. Parental involvement and concern will be reciprocated, if not in the delivery room, then a few hours, days, or even weeks afterward. If this were not the case, adoptive families would be incapable of the degree of close attachment that often develops in the absence of any birth experience whatsoever.

We have reached a stage in the development of our childbirthing practices in which the vast majority of infants can be planned for and safely born. How we approach the next area of responsibility—caring for this seemingly fragile but already amazingly complex human being—is the only real issue. Whether or not the lights are dimmed for delivery, at what moment the umbilical cord is cut, and when the baby is put to the breast must, in the final analysis, be secondary considerations.

Gentle birth is a state of mind.

Appendix A

Gentle Handling of the Newborn: An ASPO Statement*

In June 1974, the American Society for Psychoprophylaxis in Obstetrics issued the following statement on gentle handling of the newborn, here printed in its entirety:

Dr. Frederick Leboyer, a Parisian obstetrician, who wrote *Birth Without Violence,* asks us to consider birth from the baby's viewpoint. The following is a suggested protocol for couples expressing interest in Dr. Leboyer's approach to the immediate postpartum handling of babies.

Dr. Leboyer's technique is based on certain concepts which, while not proven, have some basis in animal and human research on imprinting and bonding and appear to cause no harm. These are:

1. Babies are individual human beings, capable of feeling and perhaps remembering, and whose reactions to birth and separation from the womb are unknown, but should be considered. The emotional well-being of babies as they make their transition from intrauterine life was not considered very important before Dr. Leboyer.

2. The normal baby belongs to its mother and father, not to the hospital or nursery, and we should not separate them without good reason or adequate explanation. We do not need to treat all non-medicated babies the same as sedated ones.

3. Babies do not need to cry in the early postpartum minutes to be healthy. Gentle handling and close contact with the mother appears to reduce the tendency to tense up and cry.

*Used by permission.

4. Non-medicated babies can usually handle the fluid in their respiratory tracts without deep suctioning which can cause laryngospasm and bradycardia. Bulb suctioning is quite adequate in most cases.

The application of these assumptions to the delivery room situation may proceed as follows with the prepared or lightly medicated woman who gives birth to a healthy infant.

1. The air conditioner (and blower if possible) is turned off at the time of delivery.

2. After delivery the baby can remain on the mother's abdomen until she leaves the delivery room without getting cold if:
   a. The mother dries the baby off promptly and covers him or her in a warm towel or blanket. It is recommended that the head be covered as much as possible, and stockinette caps make this easy.
   b. Skin to skin contact is encouraged after drying, to further reduce radiant heat loss.

3. The infant on its mother's abdomen seems to be comforted by gentle stroking of the back and avoiding extension (arching) of the back. The baby has been in the curled up position for months and we should not change this abruptly.

4. The nurses can do the suctioning, bracelet, footprints, vitamin K, and cord trimming on the mother's abdomen without overly exposing the baby or upsetting their routine.

5. Overhead lighting should be turned off or down right before or after delivery and the spotlight left on to complete obstetrical procedures. Then it can be directed toward the floor or wall. If lighting is dimmed, babies will open their eyes, which is much appreciated by the parents. The low lighting creates a nice mood for the miracle of birth.

6. Weighing babies in the delivery room should be discouraged because of radiant heat loss. Weighing and silver nitrate eyedrops can be done in the nursery, and the only obstacle to this is "tradition."

7. Circumcision of newborns in the delivery room should not be done.

8. If photography is desired, available light photography is less irritating to the baby than flash bulbs. Of course, the overhead lights must be turned on briefly for this. If the couple does not have the sophisticated equipment needed for available light photography, they should be permitted to use the simpler flash units, in order to have a remembrance of this most meaningful experience.

9. The baby's temperature should be checked several times during the first hour or two of life. The couples can take rectal temperatures and record them if the nurses are busy. Temperatures should be 98 degrees or more.

10. The couple may give the baby a bath before or after delivery room procedures and nursing have been completed. Local hospital routines may determine when this is done. The father may be the appropriate person to fill the infant bath tub and see that the temperature is between 98° and 100° F. Use of the radiant heater may help guard against heat loss while in the bath. Because of the time, separation, and chance for hypothermia, this feature can be played down at first or made optional.

11. Nursing may begin on the delivery table or back in the patient's labor room. Experienced mothers seem able to nurse in any position, but primiparas often find it difficult to nurse in the lithotomy position even with a wedge.

12. The mother and father are to wash their hands and arms with a germicidal soap sometime during labor, before handling their newborn baby.

Since the above steps require no special training on the part of the couple, they can be integrated into any family centered maternity care program without special permission or need to request it. By making it automatic, gentle handling of the newborn will cease to be just a fad and take its proper place as another part of modern childbirth practices.

Babies handled gently and in low light are often calm and alert only minutes after birth, looking around as if curious of their new surroundings. It is hoped that they will have a more favored start in life with a strong mother-child bond.

Appendix B

The Development of Family-Centered Maternity/Newborn Care in Hospitals * †

PREAMBLE

The Interprofessional Task Force on Health Care of Women and Children endorses the concept of family-centered maternity care as an acceptable approach to maternal/newborn care. The Task Force believes it would be beneficial to offer further comment and guidance to facilitate the implementation of such care. To this end, the organizations constituting the Task Force have participated in a multidisciplinary effort to develop a joint statement regarding the rationale behind and the practical implementation of family-centered maternity/newborn care. The effort has resulted in the development of this document, which the parent organizations believe can be helpful to those institutions considering or already implementing such programs. A description of potential components of family-centered maternity/newborn care is presented to assist implementation as judged appropriate at the local level.

DEFINITION: FAMILY-CENTERED MATERNITY/NEWBORN CARE

Family-centered maternity/newborn care can be defined as the delivery of safe, quality health care while recognizing, focusing on, and adapting to both the physical and psychosocial needs of the client-patient, the

---

* Prepared by Interprofessional Task Force on Health Care of Women and Children.
† Used by permission.

family, and the newly born. The emphasis is on the provision of maternity/newborn health care which fosters family unity while maintaining physical safety.

POSITION STATEMENT

The Task Force organizations, The American College of Obstetricians and Gynecologists, the American College of Nurse-Midwives, The Nurses Association of The American College of Obstetricians and Gynecologists, the American Academy of Pediatrics, and the American Nurses' Association, endorse the philosophy of family-centered maternity/newborn care. The development of this conviction is based upon a recognition that health includes not only physical dimensions, but social, economic and psychologic dimensions as well. Therefore, health care delivery, to be effective and satisfying for providers and the community alike, does well to acknowledge all these dimensions by adhering to the following philosophy:

— That the family is the basic unit of society;
— That the family is viewed as a whole unit within which each member is an individual enjoying recognition and entitled to consideration;
— That childbearing and childrearing are unique and important functions of the family;
— That childbearing is an experience that is appropriate and beneficial for the family to share as a unit;
— That childbearing is a developmental opportunity and/or a situational crisis, during which the family members benefit from the supporting solidarity of the family unit.

To this end, the family-centered philosophy and delivery of maternal and newborn care is important in assisting families to cope with the childbearing experience and to achieve their own goals within the concept of a high level of wellness, and within the context of the cultural atmosphere of their choosing.

The implementation of family-centered care includes recognition that the provision of maternity/newborn care requires a team effort of the woman and her family, health care providers, and the community. The composition of the team may vary from setting to setting and include obstetricians, pediatricians, family physicians, certified nurse-midwives, nurse practitioners, and other nurses. While physicians are responsible for providing direction for medical management, other team members share appropriately in managing the health care of the family, and each team member must be individually accountable for the performance of his/her facet of care. The team concept includes the cooperative inter-relationships of hospitals, health care providers, and the community in an organized system of care so as to provide for the total spectrum of maternity/newborn care within a particular geographic region.[1]

As programs are planned, it is the joint responsibility of all health professionals and their organizations involved with maternity/newborn care, through their assumptions and with input from the community, to establish guidelines for family-centered maternal and newborn care and to assure that such care will be made available to the community regard-less of economic status. It is the joint concern and responsibility of the professional organizations to commit themselves to the delivery of ma-ternal and newborn health care in settings where maximum physical safety and psychological well-being for mother and child can be assured. With these requirements met, the hospital setting provides the maxi-mum opportunity for physical safety and for psychological well-being. The development of a family-centered philosophy and implementation of the full range of this family-centered care within innovative and safe hospital settings provides the community/family with the optimum ser-vices they desire, request and need.

In view of these insights and convictions, it is recommended that each hospital obstetric, pediatric, and family practice department choosing this approach designate a joint committee on family-centered maternity/newborn care encompassing all recognized and previously stated avail-able team members, including the community. The mission of this com-mittee would be to develop, implement, and regularly evaluate a positive and comprehensive plan for family-centered maternity/newborn care in that hospital.

In addition, it is recommended that all of this be accomplished in the context of joint support for:

— The published standards as presented by The American College of Obstetricians and Gynecologists, The American College of Nurse-Midwives, The Nurses Association of The American Col-lege of Obstetricians and Gynecologists, The American Academy of Pediatrics, and the American Nurses' Association.[2,3,4,5,6,7]
— The implementation of the recommendations for the regional planning of maternal and perinatal health services, as appropriate for each region.
— The availability of a family-centered maternity/newborn service at all levels of maternity care within the regional perinatal network.

[1] Committee on Perinatal Health, The National Foundation-March of Dimes. *Toward Im-proving the Outcome of Pregnancy: Recommendations for the Regional Development of Maternal and Perinatal Health Services,* 1976.
[2] The American College of Obstetricians and Gynecologists. *Standards for Obstetric-Gyneco-logic Services,* 1974.

POTENTIAL COMPONENTS OF FAMILY-CENTERED MATERNITY/NEWBORN CARE

No specific or detailed plan for implementation of family-centered maternity/newborn care is uniformly applicable, although general guidance as to the potential components of such care is commonly sought. The following description is intended to help those who seek such guidance and is not meant to be uniformly recommended for all maternity/newborn hospital units. The attitudes and needs of the community and the providers vary from geographic area to geographic area, and economic constraints may substantially modify the utilization of each component. The detailed implementation in each hospital unit should be left to that hospital's multidisciplinary committee established to deal with such development. In addition to the maternal/newborn health care team, community and hospital administrative input should be assured. In this manner, each hospital unit can best balance community needs within economic reality.

The major change in maternity/newborn units needed in order to make family-centered care work is attitudinal. Nevertheless, a description of the potential physical and functional components of family-centered care is useful. It remains for each hospital unit to implement those components judged feasible for that unit.

I. PREPARATION OF FAMILIES: The unit should provide preparation for childbirth classes taught by appropriately prepared health professionals. Whenever possible, physicians and hospital maternity nurses should participate in such programs so as to maximize cohesion of the team providing education and care. All class approaches should include a bibliography of reading materials. The objectives of these classes are as follows:

A. To increase the community's awareness of their responsibility toward ensuring a healthy outcome for mother and child.
B. To serve as opportunities for the community and providers to

[3] American College of Nurse-Midwives. *Functions, Standards, and Qualifications,* 1975.
[4] The Nurses Association of The American College of Obstetricians and Gynecologists. *Obstetric, Gynecologic and Neonatal Nursing Functions and Standards,* 1975.
[5] American Academy of Pediatrics. *Standards and Recommendations for Hospital Care of Newborn Infants,* 1977.
[6] American Nurses' Association. *Standards of Maternal-Child Health Nursing Practice,* 1973.
[7] (a). The American College of Obstetricians and Gynecologists, the American College of Nurse-Midwives, and The Nurses Association of The American College of Obstetricians and Gynecologists. *Joint Statement on Maternity Care,* 1971.
   (b). The American College of Obstetricians and Gynecologists, the American College of Nurse-Midwives, and The Nurses Association of The American College of Obstetricians and Gynecologists. *Supplement to Joint Statement on Maternity Care,* 1975.

match expectations and achieve mutual goals from the childbirth experience.

C. To serve to assist the community to be eligible for participation
in the full family-centered program.

D. To include a tour of the hospital's maternity and newborn units.
The tour should be offered as an integral part of the preparation for childbirth programs and be available to the community
by appointment. The public should be informed of a mechanism for emergency communication with the maternity/
newborn unit.

II. PREPARATION OF HOSPITAL STAFF: A continuing education program
should be conducted on an ongoing basis to educate *all levels* of
hospital personnel who either directly or indirectly come in contact
with the family-centered program. This education program may
include:

— Content of local preparation for childbirth classes.
— Current trends in childbirth practices.
— Alternative childbirth practices: safe and unsafe, as they are
being practiced.
— Needs of childbearing families to share the total experience.
— Ways to support those families experiencing less than optimal
outcome of pregnancy.
— Explanation of term "family" so that it includes any "significant"
or "supporting other" individual to the expectant mother.
— The advantages to families and to the larger society of establish-
ing the parenting bond immediately after birth.
— The responsibilities of the patients toward ensuring a healthy
outcome of the childbirth experience.
— The potential long-term economic advantage to the hospital for
initiating the program and how this could benefit each employee.
— The satisfaction to be gained by each employee while assisting
families to adjust to the new family member.
— How the family-centered program is to function and the role
each employee is to perform to ensure its success.

III. FAMILY-CENTERED PROGRAM WITHIN THE MATERNITY/NEWBORN
UNIT: The husband or "supporting other" can remain with the
patient throughout the childbirth process as much as possible.
Family-newborn interaction immediately after birth is encouraged.

A. *Family Waiting Room* and Early Labor Lounge, attractively painted and furnished, should be available in or near the obstetrical suite where:

1. Patients in early labor could walk and visit with children, husbands, and others.
2. The husband or "supporting other" person could go for a "rest break" if necessary.
3. Access to light nourishment should be available for the husband or "supporting other."
4. Reading materials are available.
5. Telephone/intercom connections with the labor area are available.

B. *A Diagnostic-Admitting Room* should be adjacent to or near the Family Waiting Room where:
   1. Women could be examined to ascertain their status in labor without being formally admitted if they are in early labor.
   2. Any woman patient past 20 weeks gestation could be evaluated for emergency health problems during pregnancy.

C. *"Birthing Room":*
   1. A combination labor and delivery room for patient and the husband or "supporting other" during a normal labor and delivery.
   2. A brightly and attractively decorated and furnished room designed to enhance a homelike atmosphere. A comfortable lounge chair is useful.
   3. Stocked for medical emergencies for mother and infant with equipment concealed behind wall cabinets or drapes, but readily available when needed.
   4. Wired for music or intercom as desired.
   5. Equipped with a modern labor-delivery bed which can be:
      (a). raised and lowered.
      (b). adjusted to semi-sitting position.
      (c). moved to the delivery room if the need arises.
   6. Equipped with a cribbette with warmer and have the capacity for infant resuscitation.
   7. Appropriately supplied for a normal spontaneous vaginal delivery and the immediate care of a normal newborn.
   8. An environment in which breastfeeding and handling of the baby are encouraged immediately after delivery with due consideration given to maintaining the baby's normal temperature.

D. *Labor Rooms:*
1. The husband or "supporting other" can be with a laboring patient whether progress in labor is normal or abnormal.
2. Regulation hospital equipment is available.
3. An emergency delivery can be performed.
4. Attention is given to the surroundings which are attractively furnished and include a comfortable lounge chair.

E. *Delivery Rooms:* Should be properly equipped with standard items but, in addition, should have delivery tables with adjustable backrests. An overhead mirror should be available. The delivery rooms should accommodate breastfeeding and handling of the baby after delivery with due consideration to maintaining the baby's normal temperature.

F. *Recovery Room:* Patients may be returned from the delivery room to their original labor rooms, depending upon the demand, or to a recovery room. Such a recovery room should have all the standard equipment but also allow for the following options:
1. The infant to be allowed to be with the mother and father or "supporting other" for a time period after delivery with due consideration given to the infant's physiologic adjustment to extrauterine life. Where feasible, post-caesarean section patients may be allowed the same option.
2. The husband or "supporting other" to be allowed to visit with the new mother and baby with some provision for privacy.
3. A "pass" to be given to the father or "supporting other" of the baby to allow for extended visiting privileges on the "new family unit."

G. The Postpartum *"new Family Unit"* should:
1. Contain flexible rooming-in with a central nursery to allow:
   (a). Optional "rooming-in."
   (b). Babies to be returned to the central nursery for professional nursing care when desired by the mother.
   (c). Maximum desired maternal/infant contact especially during the first 24 hours.
2. Have extended visiting hours for the father or "supporting other" to provide the opportunity to assist with the care and feeding of the baby.
3. Have limited visiting hours for friends since the emphasis of the family-centered approach is on the family.

4. Contain a family room where:
   (a). Children can visit with their mothers and fathers.
   (b). Professional staff are available to answer questions about parenting and issues regarding adjustments to the enlarged family.
   (c). Cafeteria-like meals can be served and eaten restaurant-style by the mothers.
5. Have group and individual instruction provided by appropriately prepared personnel on postpartum care, family planning, infant feeding, infant care and parenting.
6. Allow visiting and feeding by the mothers in the special nurseries such as:
   (a). Newborn, intensive care nursery.
   (b). Isolation nursery.
7. Allow for breastfeeding/bottle feeding on demand with professional personnel available for assistance.

H. Discharge planning should include options for early discharge. If this option is desired, careful attention to continuing medical and/or nursing contact after discharge to ensure maternal and newborn health is important. Potential for utilization of appropriate referral systems should be available.

Additional copies may be obtained from the offices of each participating organization or from the Interprofessional Task Force Secretariat, ACOG, One East Wacker Drive, Suite 2700, Chicago, Illinois 60601.

American Academy of Pediatrics
Robert T. Hall, M.D.
Lawrence Kahn, M.D.
Mary Kaye Willian, R.N., P.N.A.

American College of Nurse-Midwives
Helen V. Burst, C.N.M., M.S.
Betty J. Carrington, C.N.M., M.S.
Dorothea M. Lang, C.N.M., M.P.H.

*American College of
Obstetricians and Gynecologists*
Richard H. Aubry, M.D., Chairman
Ervin E. Nichols, M.D.
Warren H. Pearse, M.D.
William O. Thomas, Jr., M.D.

American Nurses' Association
Ann L. Clark, R.N., M.A.
Beverly R. Mulder, R.N., S.N.P., M.S.

*Nurses Association of The American College of
Obstetricians and Gynecologists*
Barbara V. Bland, R.N.C.
Sallye P. Brown, R.N., B.S.N., M.N.
Bonnie Wiltse, R.N., B.S.
Ruth Young, R.N., B.S.N.

This position statement has also been endorsed by the American Hospital Association.

Suggestions for Further Reading

Scientific and anecdotal material found in *The Gentle Birth Book* was derived from over a hundred published sources, as well as dozens of personal and telephone interviews. Faced with a choice of including all— and overwhelming the reader with a barrage of unedited information —or selecting a limited number of thought-provoking, highly readable books on a range of related topics, we selected the latter course. Although some of the opinions presented in the following texts will naturally differ from our own, each in its own way is a good source book for the expectant parent or anyone else interested in this formative stage in human development.

Annis, Linda F. *The Child Before Birth.* Ithaca and London: Cornell University Press, 1978.

Bean, Constance A. *Methods of Childbirth.* Garden City, N.Y.: Doubleday, 1972.

Bing, Elisabeth. *Six Practical Lessons for an Easier Birth.* New York: Grosset and Dunlap, 1967.

Bradley, Robert A. *Husband-Coached Childbirth.* New York: Harper & Row, 1974.

Brazelton, T. Berry. *Infants and Mothers: Differences in Development.* New York: Delacorte Press, 1969.

Chabon, Irwin. *Awake and Aware.* New York: Delacorte Press, 1969.

Eiger, Marvin, and Olds, Sally W. *The Complete Book of Breastfeeding.* New York: Workman, 1972.

Elkins, Valmai H. *The Rights of the Pregnant Parent.* New York: Two Continents, 1976.

Fraiberg, Selma. *Every Child's Birthright: In Defense of Mothering.* New York: Basic Books, 1977.

Kaplan, Louise J. *Oneness and Separateness: From Infant to Individual.* New York: Simon & Schuster, 1978.

Klaus, Marshall H., and Kennell, John H. *Maternal-Infant Bonding.* St. Louis: C. V. Mosby, 1976.

Leach, Penelope. *Your Baby and Child: From Birth to Age Five.* New York: Alfred A. Knopf, 1978.

Leboyer, Frederick. *Birth Without Violence.* New York: Alfred A. Knopf, 1975.

Leidloff, Jean. *The Continuum Concept.* New York: Alfred A. Knopf, 1977.

Macfarlane, Aidan. *The Psychology of Childbirth.* Cambridge, Mass.: Harvard University Press, 1977.

Pryor, Karen. *Nursing Your Baby.* Rev. ed. New York: Harper & Row, 1973.

Salk, Lee, and Kramer, Rita. *How to Raise a Human Being.* New York: Random House, 1969.

Schaffer, Rudolph. *Mothering.* Cambridge, Mass.: Harvard University Press, 1977.

Segal, Julius, and Yahraes, Herbert. *A Child's Journey: Forces That Shape the Lives of Our Young.* New York: McGraw-Hill, 1978.

Stern, Daniel. *The First Relationship.* Cambridge, Mass.: Harvard University Press, 1977.

ABOUT THE AUTHORS

NANCY BEREZIN considered teaching literature or medieval history, then wandered into medical publishing and stayed. Great-granddaughter of a rural "horse-and-buggy" doctor, she is the author of numerous articles on current developments in obstetrics/gynecology and pediatrics. This is her first full-length book.

JOHN W. GROVER, M.D., formerly of Harvard Medical School and the Boston Hospital for Women, is currently chairman of the department of obstetrics and gynecology at Lutheran General Hospital, Park Ridge, Illinois. In addition to the film *Gentle Birth,* Dr. Grover's film credits include the classic *Not Me Alone.*

JOHN S. ROBEY, M.D., is clinical instructor in pediatrics, Harvard Medical School, and associate pediatrician, Massachusetts General Hospital.